WOMEN
of the
CHRISTIAN
FAITH

The
TOP 100
WOMEN
of the
CHRISTIAN
FAITH

Who They Are and
What They Mean to You Today

JEWELL JOHNSON

BARBOUR
PUBLISHING

© 2009 by Barbour Publishing, Inc.

Print ISBN 978-1-61626-682-0

eBook Editions:
Adobe Digital Edition (.epub) 978-1-62029-678-3
Kindle and MobiPocket Edition (.prc) 978-1-62029-677-6

Scripture quotations marked kjv are taken from the King James Version of the Bible.

Scripture quotations marked niv are taken from the HOLY BIBLE, NEW INTERNATIONAL VERSION®. niv®. Copyright © 1973, 1978, 1984 by International Bible Society. Used by permission of Zondervan. All rights reserved.

Scripture quotations marked nlt are taken from the *Holy Bible*, New Living Translation, copyright © 1996. Used by permission of Tyndale House Publishers, Inc. Wheaton, Illinois 60189, U.S.A. All rights reserved.

Scripture quotations marked THE MESSAGE are from *THE MESSAGE*. Copyright © by Eugene H. Peterson 1993, 1994, 1995, 1996, 2000, 2001, 2002. Used by permission of NavPress Publishing Group.

Cover image: Tetra Images/Getty

Published by Barbour Publishing, Inc., P.O. Box 719, Uhrichsville, Ohio 44683, www.barbourbooks.com

Our mission is to publish and distribute inspirational products offering exceptional value and biblical encouragement to the masses.

Member of the
Evangelical Christian
Publishers Association

Printed in the United States of America.

CONTENTS

INTRODUCTION

"We are surrounded by such a great cloud of witnesses," the writer of Hebrews tells us (Hebrews 12:1 NIV). Included in this crowd are the Christian women whose names fill the pages of this book: missionaries, songwriters, pastors' wives, preachers, evangelists, housewives, and businesswomen. Some of their beliefs and activities were controversial in their time— and could still be today. But each has a message for us. What they did and how they lived their lives speaks to us today.

Some of these women have passed on. Others remain. These hundred women did a variety of work as they labored for good causes. Although some died young, such as Mary Ann Paton who died at nineteen, each was productive in her own way.

One message that will come to you as you read is that God has given each of us gifts. These vary and are unique, so there is no need to be discontent with yours or envy another woman's gift. And this world desperately needs our gifts. As you read each woman's story, you will be reminded of the apostle Paul's admonition to Timothy regarding his ministry, "Keep that ablaze!" (2 Timothy 1:6 THE MESSAGE).

But the main truth these women's lives impart to us is to *be faithful*—to our families, churches, nation, and God. In spite of health problems, as in the case of Mary Lyon; in spite of the deaths of children, as Hannah Whitall Smith experienced; and even, in the face of grave disappointment in ministry, as happened to Mary McLeod Bethune when she was refused a missionary appointment to Africa *twice*, these women were faithful to overcome every obstacle to use their gifts.

We don't struggle alone—others have run the race before us. They patiently endured suffering, overcame temptations, and, using their gifts, completed the work assigned to them. They won! And you and I will, too, as we "fix our eyes on Jesus."

Take a few moments each day to ponder the scripture verse that introduces each woman's story. Listen to what each faithful woman says. Pray about the messages you hear. And ask God to help you also be a faithful witness.

ANN HASSELTINE JUDSON

Missionary (1789–1826)

*"I am the Lord's servant, and I am willing
to accept whatever he wants."*
LUKE 1:38 NLT

At age sixteen, Ann Hasseltine wrote in her journal, "Only let me know Thy will, and I will readily comply." Five years later, she met Adoniram Judson. The two fell in love, and a day after their wedding in 1812, the couple sailed for missionary service in India.

The Judsons were not allowed to enter India, however, and instead went to Burma. Ann learned the language, translated the book of Jonah into Burmese, and opened a school for girls. During that time, she gave birth to a son who, at eight months, died of jungle fever.

When a war broke out, Adoniram was arrested and tortured. Ann, pregnant with their second child, brought her husband food and pled for his release. During his almost two-year imprisonment, she gave birth to the child and endured horrendous conditions to minister to her husband. Soon after Adoniram's release, Ann died of spotted fever.

Did Ann's earlier commitment bear any fruit? Her short life inspired others to accept the challenges of difficult mission fields—and sixty years after her death, Burma had sixty-three churches served by 163 workers.

God's work advances through the dedicated lives of His people—people who place no restrictions on God, who rather say, "I am willing to accept whatever You want."

MARY MCLEOD BETHUNE

Christian Educator (1875–1955)

Do not be anxious about anything,
but in everything, by prayer and petition,
with thanksgiving, present your requests to God.
PHILIPPIANS 4:6 NIV

Mary McLeod, one of seventeen children born to ex-slaves, became a Christian and learned to pray at a young age. When she asked her father if she could attend school, he said there were no schools for black children. But one day a missionary teacher appeared at the McLeod cabin and announced she was starting a school. Mary's father gave his permission for her to attend.

After each school day, the family gathered as Mary told them what she had learned. She also began helping neighbors with reading and arithmetic. Mary graduated from the mission school at age twelve, yet her heart yearned for more education. The family had no money—and when their mule dropped dead, Mary, with other family members, took turns pulling a plow.

Then a miracle happened. A Quaker woman donated money to allow a black child to attend a school in North Carolina. Mary was chosen for the scholarship and attended seven years. Later she went to Moody Bible Institute, the only black student on campus. Upon graduation, Mary felt called to take the gospel to Africa. But when she applied to a mission board, they rejected her—not once, but twice. She said, "It was the greatest disappointment of my life."

Consumed with a desire to help black women have a better life, Mary began a school in her home for five girls. The school grew, and Mary founded Daytona Normal and Industrial School for Girls. Money was scarce, and Mary went from house to house begging for funds. Using her fine singing voice, she also held concerts.

The Ku Klux Klan didn't like Mary's bold stand for blacks voting in public elections—and one night, eighty hooded men rode up to the school carrying torches, threatening to burn the buildings. Mary told them, "If you burn my buildings, I'll build them again. If you burn them a second time, I'll build them again." Then she and the students sang, "Be not dismayed what-e'er betide; God will take care of you." The white hoods slipped away.

Mary was appointed to various government posts during the terms of Presidents Calvin Coolidge, Herbert Hoover, and Franklin Roosevelt. From 1936 to 1944, she served as director of the Division of Negro Affairs of the National Youth Administration, the first black woman to head a federal agency.

At an early age, Mary learned to trust God—and her faith, coupled with prayer, sustained her for a lifetime. God promises to do the same for anyone who believes, prays, and trusts Him to provide.

ELIZABETH KA'AHUMANU

Hawaiian Queen (1768–1832)

*Those who become Christians become new persons. . .
the old life is gone. A new life has begun!*
2 CORINTHIANS 5:17 NLT

After Ka'ahumanu became a Christian, her subjects referred
to her as the "new Ka'ahumanu." But their queen's conversion did not come without a struggle.

When missionaries first came to Hawaii around 1820,
Ka'ahumanu listened to their message. She attended their
schools. But abandon her idols and accept their God? She
hesitated.

Ka'ahumanu had married at age thirteen and became
one of the many wives of King Kamehameha. Soon after
their marriage, the king died and Ka'ahumanu married his
son. He also died, leaving Ka'ahumanu queen regnant of
the Hawaiian Islands.

For four years, Ka'ahumanu carefully weighed her decision. When she converted to Christianity in 1824, the
change was drastic. She publicly embraced Christianity
and encouraged her subjects to do the same. Before she
was baptized, she instituted new laws based on the Ten
Commandments. She also ordered the pagan idols to be
torn down and destroyed the sugar cane fields to stop the
production of rum. No wonder citizens of Hawaii called
her the "new Ka'ahumanu"!

Salvation is not a reformation or a rehabilitation program. When we believe in Jesus, we receive a new heart.

Hawaiians noted the gospel's power to change their queen, and a watching world also notices when we find a brand-new life in Christ.

FRANCES RIDLEY HAVERGAL

Hymn Writer, Author (1836–79)

> " 'Love the Lord your God with all your heart
> and with all your soul and with all your mind.'
> This is the first and greatest commandment."
> MATTHEW 22:37–38 NIV

Frances Havergal read French, Greek, and Hebrew. She was an accomplished pianist and had a well-trained voice. Frances was also a vibrant Christian, possessing a simple faith and unwavering joy.

Frances was born in England. Her father, a Church of England minister, was a musician as well who wrote over one hundred hymns. A bright child, Frances was educated at home and could read by age three. She developed a love for the scriptures as a youngster, possibly because her father held her on his lap each day as he read from the Bible. At age four she began memorizing Bible verses, and was soon writing poetry.

Frances's happy home life was disrupted when her mother became seriously sick. After a long illness, she died, leaving Frances, her four sisters, and a brother. Frances said of that time, "A mother's death must be childhood's greatest grief."

As a child, Frances was especially intrigued by the communion service. Because children were not allowed at the Lord's Supper, she would listen through the vestry door, counting the years until she could at last take part in the sacrament.

Her conversion experience began with a deep sense of sinfulness. Frances would lie in bed and cry, pondering how wicked she was. At that time she attended a private school. Mrs. Teed, a godly teacher, told the girls both in class and privately of their need of the Savior. As a result, several girls were saved. When a fellow student testified of her great joy, Frances experienced what she called a "revival"—she was genuinely converted to Jesus.

Thus Frances entered into a life of deep dedication to Christ. She maintained a disciplined devotional life, praying three times a day, taking a topic such as forgiveness or watchfulness for each prayer time.

After her father remarried, Frances accompanied him and his new wife to Germany in 1852. There she saw a painting of Christ's crucifixion and read the words engraved beneath: THIS I HAVE DONE FOR THEE; WHAT HAST THOU DONE FOR ME? Moved by the words and the painting, she wrote the poem, "I Gave My Life for Thee." Later she read the verses and, in disgust, decided they did not convey what her heart felt. She crumpled the paper and threw it in the fire, only to have it leap from the flames to the floor. Frances showed the verses to her father, who wrote a melody for the words.

I gave My life for thee; My precious blood I shed,
That thou might ransomed be, And quickened from the dead.
I gave, I gave My life for thee, What hast thou giv'n for Me?

Another of Frances's hymns, "Take My Life," came about when she spent five days visiting a friend's house. Ten other people were also guests in the home, and Frances, at the onset of the visit, prayed, "Lord, give me all in this house!" Before the guests left, each person had received a blessing in answer to her prayer. On the last night of the visit, Frances, too excited to sleep, praised God and renewed her consecration. Soon words came to her and she wrote, "Take my life and let it be, consecrated, Lord, to Thee."

Always frail in health, in 1879 Frances caught a cold that escalated into a lung infection. When she was told her life was in danger, she said, "That's too good to be true." Her sister, Maria, writing of her sister's last moments, said Frances began to sing "Golden Harps Are Sounding," a song she had written. "There was a radiance on her face," Maria said. "It was as though she had already seen the Lord."

Through Frances Havergal's life and the verses she wrote, we catch a glimpse into the heart of a deeply spiritual person. Today her hymns call us to live fervently for Jesus so our deaths will also be a simple transition into the presence of our best Friend.

HANNAH MORE

Author, Teacher (1745–1833)

I have become all things to all men so that
by all possible means I might save some.
I do all this for the sake of the gospel,
that I may share in its blessings.
1 CORINTHIANS 9:22–23 NIV

As a young adult, Hannah More wrote plays for the theater and mingled with England's elite. But at age thirty-five, her attention shifted, and she became friends with hymn writer John Newton and Christian statesman William Wilberforce.

One day Hannah accompanied Wilberforce to a mining district. After seeing the needs of the poverty-stricken families, she established a Sunday school for the children and gave them Bibles and clothing. With her sister, she organized Sunday schools that eventually instructed as many as twenty thousand children.

Not willing to leave one stone unturned to reach people for Christ, Hannah created a pamphlet, called a tract, in which she did battle with the promoters of atheism and the political radicals of the day. In 1795, she published three tracts a month. In one year, she reported selling over two million tracts.

How will the people of our communities be won for Christ? As members of Christ's body, when we use our talents to do what we can, every person around us will feel God's love and be challenged to serve the Savior.

GRACIA BURNHAM

Missionary (1959–)

*Even though I walk through the valley of the shadow of death,
I will fear no evil, for you are with me.*
PSALM 23:4 NIV

Gracia and Martin Burnham, missionaries in the Philippines,
were celebrating their eighteenth wedding anniversary at an
island resort when, early one morning, they were awakened
by a banging on their door. Before Martin could open the
door, three men with M16 rifles charged into the room yell-
ing, "Go! Go!" The Burnhams, with other resort guests,
were herded onto a speedboat, hostages of an Islamic group
called Abu Sayyaf. With only the few clothes she was wearing, Gracia did not dream their captivity would stretch into a
year, ending with her husband's death.

Gracia and Martin met at Calvary Bible College in
Kansas City. After their marriage in 1983, the couple
applied for missionary service—and when the New Tribes
Mission needed a pilot in the Philippines, the Burnhams
were appointed.

They lived on the northern island of Luzon where
Martin flew supplies to missionary families. Gracia kept in
contact with him and the missionaries by radio. Soon three
children joined their family.

That day in May 2001, Gracia and Martin's captors
demanded large sums of money for their safe return—but
in the meantime they hid them at gunpoint in the jungle.
As the hostages were moved to avoid contact with Filipino

military forces, food and water were often scarce. On one occasion the Burnhams went nine days without a meal, eating only leaves. With poor food and water sources, Gracia and Martin struggled with intestinal problems. The jungle marches were often at night. When they slept, it was on the ground with Martin chained to a tree.

Besides the physical suffering, the Burnhams endured intense mental agony. Occasionally packages arrived from family members, but the food was taken by their captors. Although Gracia and Martin were frequently promised a release, the promises never materialized. As the captivity continued, Gracia experienced depression and Martin's weight dropped drastically.

Gracia didn't always feel God near during her captivity, but she and Martin never doubted His presence. Although they had no Bible, they encouraged each other with scripture verses and prayed together daily.

On June 7, 2002, the Filipino military closed in around the Abu Sayyaf and their hostages. A gun battle ensued. As Gracia and Martin ran, she was shot in the leg and he in the chest. Gracia was rescued, but Martin died.

While we may not be held hostage by enemy forces, we all have experiences in which we feel estranged from God. The Bible assures us that God does not leave us in our valleys. That is our comfort as we face perilous times.

MORROW GRAHAM

Housewife, Mother (1892–1981)

Let the word of Christ dwell in you richly
as you teach and admonish one another with all wisdom.
COLOSSIANS 3:16 NIV

"There's only one right way to live," Morrow Graham said, "and it's all laid out in the Bible." She also believed the prayers of a mother greatly influence her children's choices.

Morrow's prayers evidently made a difference in the life of her oldest son, Billy Graham, who has preached in more than 185 countries; reached millions through radio, television, and film; and counseled heads of governments.

When Morrow married Frank Graham in 1916, they moved to a North Carolina farm. On the first day of their marriage, they established a family altar—a time of Bible reading and prayer. The Grahams ran a dairy farm, rising at 2:30 in the morning to milk as many as seventy-five cows. In spite of a hectic schedule, before they ate, Frank prayed a blessing on the food—and at breakfast, Morrow read a verse from a scripture calendar. As she packed the children's lunches, her husband helped them memorize Bible verses. In the evening, the family gathered to read the Bible and pray.

Morrow, a busy housewife, gave priority to the basics, and it paid big dividends for her family and the world. When we make eternal matters the priority, our families will also reap a spiritual harvest for generations to come.

HANNAH WHITALL SMITH

Author, Bible Teacher (1832–1911)

*"You will seek me and find me when
you seek me with all your heart."*
JEREMIAH 29:13 NIV

Hannah Whitall Smith wasn't afraid to ask God difficult questions. As she searched, she found answers and shared them in her book *The Christian's Secret of a Happy Life*.

When the book appeared in print in 1875, it immediately became a bestseller and was translated into every European language and a number of Asian languages. The book remains popular today.

Hannah was born into a Quaker family in Philadelphia. Her father, a wealthy glass manufacturer, provided his daughter with a happy childhood. As a young adult, Hannah studied the scriptures and made an astounding discovery: Christ was her salvation. No amount of good works placed her in right standing with God. He didn't love her more because she wore plain clothes or refrained from wearing jewelry. With this discovery, the Bible became a new book to Hannah—and she declared Christ's salvation should not make one miserable, but rather, happy.

Hannah married Robert Smith, also a Quaker, and together they preached and led Bible studies. When they moved to Millville, New Jersey, the couple caused a stir in their families when they abandoned the Quaker persuasion for the holiness movement. Hannah's father, usually good-natured, commanded the couple to leave his house.

She wrote of that time, ". . .like an outcast from my earthly father's house. But not from my heavenly Father's house."

Early in her Christian life, Hannah became extremely concerned for people who did not know Christ as their Savior. One day while riding a streetcar, she became burdened for two passengers. Hannah pulled her veil tightly around her face to hide her anguish. A Voice assured her, "It is not My will that any should perish." The burden lifted and a relieved Hannah stepped off the streetcar.

When Hannah and Robert moved to Millville, Hannah missed her friends in the Bible study she had attended in Pennsylvania. Her pastor suggested she befriend the poor people in her neighborhood. She accepted an invitation from her dressmaker to attend a testimony meeting. Hannah, feeling her grasp of Bible knowledge superior to that of factory workers, wondered what the congregation could teach her. A woman with a shawl on her head rose and confessed that her life used to be filled with "this big me." But after receiving a vision of her humble Savior, "this big me, melted to nothing." Humbled by the words, and aware of a prideful heart, Hannah concluded that "this was real Christianity, the kind I long for."

Hannah and Robert had five children. When their five-year-old daughter died from a bronchial condition, Hannah could not be consoled. That summer, the family spent their vacation at a beach, and Hannah took only one book with her—the Bible. Day after day she read, searching for comfort. One day it happened. She rose from her chair and shouted, "I believe. Oh, Lord, I believe!" As a result of this experience, Hannah wrote the book *The God of All Comfort*.

While the couple preached in England, Hannah was

plunged into despair upon learning that Robert had an extramarital affair. Rejection and shame threatened her peace of mind. Again she sought God's answers in the Bible. She came to the conclusion that God was enough for her lonely heart. Not His gifts or blessings, but God Himself was enough for life at its best and at its lowest points. She told a friend, dejected because she was not married, "Thy loneliness is the loneliness of a heart made for God. I am determined I will be satisfied with God alone."

Questions! Life is full of them. Hannah found answers in the Bible, and Christian believers also know where to go when facing life's complex, seemingly unanswerable questions. As we pray and search His Word, God may give us insight into the "whys." However, sometimes the answer will not be revealed to us. In these instances, we rest in His peace knowing the answers are not as important as having a faith that remains steady when facing life's storms.

CHARLOTTE ELLIOTT

Hymn Writer (1789–1871)

For Christ's sake, I delight in weaknesses, in insults,
in hardships, in persecutions, in difficulties.
For when I am weak, then I am strong.
2 CORINTHIANS 12:10 NIV

One day a minister asked Charlotte Elliot if she was a Christian. Depressed because of ill health, she informed him she did not want to discuss religion. A few days later, Charlotte thought about the minister's question. She went to him and said, "I want to be saved, but I don't know how."

"Come to Him just as you are," he replied. That day Charlotte received Jesus into her heart. Fourteen years later, as she thought about those words, she wrote the now-popular invitation hymn, "Just as I Am."

Charlotte's health did not improve, yet she continued to write hymns. She compiled *The Invalid's Hymn Book*—and after several editions, the hymnbook eventually contained one hundred of Charlotte's songs.

The last fifty years of her life, Charlotte was confined to her home. Her brother, a pastor, said he had some results from his ministry, but Charlotte's one hymn saw more fruit than all his sermons.

God didn't remove Charlotte's physical afflictions; rather, He used her *in* her weakness. We, too, may face obstacles that attempt to deter us from doing a work for God, but in our weakness—relying on His strength—we can bless others.

CORETTA SCOTT KING

Author, Activist, Civil Rights Leader (1927–2006)

Live in harmony with one another;
be sympathetic, love as brothers. . . .
Do not repay evil with evil or insult with insult,
but with blessing.
1 PETER 3:8–9 NIV

Martin Luther King Jr. was killed in April 1968, near the anniversary of Jesus' death and resurrection. Remembering her Savior's death, Coretta King was comforted. Dare she hope her husband's death would also bring comfort to the world's downtrodden?

Coretta Scott grew up in Marian, Alabama. Early in life, she noticed white children rode buses to school while she and other black children walked. She and her friends attended school seven months of the year. The white children attended nine months.

Coretta's sister attended Antioch College in Ohio—and when Coretta applied for a scholarship, she was accepted. Life was different for her in the North. She noticed there were no WHITES ONLY and COLORED ONLY signs on public buildings. She could eat in local restaurants and walk in any city park.

At Antioch, Coretta began giving concerts in churches and decided to further her musical studies. She was accepted at the New England Conservatory of Music in Boston. There she met Martin Luther King Jr. who was working on a theology degree at Boston University.

They married in 1953, and Martin became a pastor in Montgomery, Alabama.

Coretta and Martin were familiar with Southern segregation laws and had reluctantly accepted the unfair treatment of their race. That changed in 1955 when a black woman, Rosa Parks, refused to give up her seat on a Montgomery bus and was arrested. Local black leaders decided to boycott the bus company, and Martin was chosen as the leader of The Montgomery Improvement Association.

Coretta and Martin agreed they would fight injustice as Jesus did: with love and compassion. When the four King children asked why they couldn't play in parks marked WHITES ONLY, Coretta told them their daddy was trying to change the unfair rules.

Not everyone believed nonviolence was the way to deal with segregation. The Kings were bombarded daily with hate mail. In 1956, Coretta heard a thud on the porch. She grabbed the baby and ran to the rear of the home as an explosion shook the building. When her husband led peaceful demonstrations, he was repeatedly arrested and jailed.

Coretta did not seek revenge for her husband's senseless murder. Rather, following Jesus' words to love her enemies, she spent her entire life working for equality for all people. Our natural response to injustice is to lash out. Coretta proved how much more effective it is to pray for those who spitefully use us, conquering hatred with Christ's love.

MARY DYER

Martyr (1611?–60)

Don't condemn each other anymore.
Decide instead to. . .not put an obstacle
in another Christian's path.
ROMANS 14:13 NLT

In 1635, Puritans Mary and William Dyer immigrated to Boston where Mary gave birth to a deformed stillborn child. When other Puritans learned Mary had "birthed a monster," they believed this was evidence of God's displeasure. As a result, Mary and her family were banished from Massachusetts Bay.

The Dyers then made a trip to England where they came in contact with George Fox, the founder of the Quakers. Mary accepted the teaching, knowing his followers were suffering persecution for their faith.

Returning to America, Mary ignored a law that banned Quakers from Boston and was arrested. She escaped death when her husband intervened. Defying the laws again, Mary returned to Boston—and when she refused to stop preaching, Governor John Endicott demanded her death. Again her husband came to her rescue. In May 1660, Mary appeared in Boston a third time, and authorities condemned her to death by hanging. Was Mary Dyer overstepping her boundaries by defying Puritan authority? Were the Puritans—who enjoyed religious freedom in America—unwilling to grant the same privilege to others? Whatever the case, Mary's death calls attention to the evils of religious intolerance. We do well to pattern our lives after Jesus, the Prince of Peace, and leave the judging to God.

GRACE LIVINGSTON HILL

Author (1865–1947)

God has given each of us the ability to do certain things well. So if God has given you the ability to prophesy, speak out when you have faith that God is speaking through you.
ROMANS 12:6 NLT

Her daughters saw her as a woman of great strength. Her readers knew her as the "Queen of the Christian Romance," the writer who single-handedly laid the foundation for the now-popular Christian romance genre.

In 1892, Grace Livingston married Frank Hill, a pastor. Within a few days of their marriage, Grace noticed Frank experienced frequent mood swings. One Sunday, while he led the church service, he suddenly left the platform. Grace followed him and saw him swallow two pills. When she questioned him, he admitted to an addiction that had begun years earlier. Treatment for addictions and rehabilitation centers were unknown in 1892.

A shadow had entered their marriage, yet Grace told no one. Seven years later, Frank died of a ruptured appendix, and Grace became the sole support of their two daughters.

A short time later, Grace's father also died, and her mother came to live with her. Now Grace was responsible to support a family of four. She assessed her skills and decided she would meet the crisis using her talent for writing.

Writing for publication was not new to Grace. Years earlier when her family was unable to afford a vacation, she had an idea for a novel. A contract came, Grace wrote *A Chautauqua Idyl*, and the family took the vacation.

As Grace seriously pursued a writing career, there was no doubt what type of novel she would write. She determined her books would carry a clear gospel message. But when she submitted a book to an editor, he rejected her manuscript, telling her to "take out the gospel. This sort of thing won't sell." Grace refused. She managed to write eight novels in the next six years. Each book depicted the struggle of good against evil and concluded with the theme of God's ability to change and restore.

People evidently needed the messages of Grace's books. She wrote over one hundred romance novels, which sold approximately one million copies in her lifetime. In addition, Grace, with Evangeline Booth, wrote a history of the Salvation Army during World War I.

"God gave me gifts," Grace said. "I will do all I can to show Him how grateful I am to Him. I'm going to spend more of my time and effort spreading Christ's gospel."

We can use our talents in selfish pursuits—or, like Grace Livingston Hill, we can find creative ways to spread the light of Christ's glorious salvation using the gifts He's given to us.

BLANDINA

Christian Martyr (?–177)

Many were amazed when they saw him—beaten and bloodied,
so disfigured one would scarcely know he was a person.
ISAIAH 52:14 NLT

To honor Rome and the emperor, the governor of Lyons
(now France) decided to entertain his citizens by torturing
Christians.

Christianity had come to the city twenty-five years
earlier—and as the church grew, Christians were shut out of
businesses, robbed, and beaten. When believers continued
to testify, they were thrown into prison.

Blandina, a slave girl, was also in prison—and that day,
she watched as hot irons were pressed on fellow Christians
and they were torn apart by wild animals. When it was her
turn, she was tied to a stake and wild beasts were released
to torment her. To the spectators' surprise, none of the
beasts touched her.

On the final day of "entertainment," Blandina was beaten
from morning until evening. Then she was thrown to a wild
bull and placed on the roasting seat until her body was one
gaping wound. In the midst of her pain, she cried out, "I am
a Christian, and there is nothing vile done by us."

The treatment Blandina received reminds us of Christ's
sufferings. Her reaction to her persecutors was similar to the
Savior's. Both endured. And we take notice, ponder, and
know we, too, will receive strength should such persecution
be our fate.

HARRIET TUBMAN

Emancipator (1820?–1913)

*"Be strong and courageous,
because you will lead these people to inherit the land
I swore to their forefathers to give them.
Be strong and very courageous."*
Joshua 1:6–7 NIV

Harriet Tubman was born into slavery on a plantation in
Maryland. One day after six-year-old Harriet had worked
all day, her owner's wife told her to care for a sick child
through the night. She fell asleep, the baby cried—and for
the remainder of her life, Harriet bore scars from the whip-
ping she received.

By the time she was eleven, she worked in the field like a
man. On one occasion, an overseer threw a metal weight at
another slave and hit Harriet, causing a head injury. For days
she hovered between life and death. When she recovered, she
suffered from headaches, seizures, and periods of uncontrol-
lable sleepiness. After the injury, she also experienced visions
and dreams that she believed came from God.

Although her parents could not read or write, Harriet's
mother told her children Bible stories and raised them to
fear God. When Harriet told her father she yearned for
freedom, he told her to trust God. She prayed that her
harsh master would become a Christian, but when that
prayer wasn't answered, Harriet asked God to take him out
of the way. She became terrified when the man died.

Harriet lived in constant fear of white people: fear of

punishment and fear of being sold into the Deep South, which had been the fate of her three sisters. When Harriet married, she shared with her husband, John, her desire for freedom—but he discouraged such talk.

In 1849, unknown to Harriet, her owner planned to sell her. Before this happened, by mysterious means, Harriet was warned to flee. Aided by a Quaker woman, Harriet and two of her brothers began the dangerous journey north. Soon the frightened brothers turned back.

Harriet traveled by night, her eye on the North Star. During the day, she hid in swamps or burrowed in holes in fields. Along the way, she stopped for food and directions at Underground Railroad homes. Slave catchers, with their vicious dogs, were a constant threat—yet Harriet vowed she would not be taken alive.

At last Harriet reached Pennsylvania, a free state. But without her family she was lonely. For a year Harriet worked and saved her money. When she received word that a niece and her young children were to be sold, Harriet did the unthinkable: She traveled south and safely guided the family to freedom. The next year, Harriet rescued her three brothers and other slaves. Later she freed her parents. Once a person agreed to escape with Harriet, there was no turning around. If a slave threatened to go back, Harriet would pull out a revolver and tell the frightened black, "You go on or die."

As a "conductor" on the Underground Railroad for eight years, Harriet experienced many narrow escapes, yet the five-foot-tall woman gave Jesus credit for each successful rescue. She boasted that she "never lost a passenger."

Slaves loved her and called her "Moses" after Israel's

deliverer from Egyptian bondage. John Brown consulted with Harriet about recruiting soldiers to help him in the raid on Harper's Ferry. Slaveholders feared Harriet and offered a reward for her dead or alive, yet she was not captured. In 1860, Harriet made her nineteenth and last trip south. She had rescued more than three hundred slaves from bondage.

During the Civil War, Harriet served in the Union Army as a cook, spy, scout, and nurse. In 1863, she led the Union Army in an armed assault along the Combahee River that liberated more than seven hundred slaves. Harriet never was paid for her services. After the war, she established homes for orphans, the aged, and the homeless.

Harriet received courage to perform dangerous exploits. While most believers aren't called to such heroism, we all face tasks that require more courage than we ordinarily possess. At these times, we can rely on God. Just at the right moment, when we need it the most, He has promised to give us all the courage we need.

DOROTHY CAREY

Missionary Wife (1755–1807)

*Who then is willing to consecrate
his service this day unto the LORD?*
1 CHRONICLES 29:5 KJV

She had willingly served with her husband in small Baptist
churches in England—but when William announced his
plans to go as a missionary to India, Dorothy Carey refused
to go. Though uneducated, she was aware of the dangers
she'd face in a foreign country. And there were her children to
consider. She had three young sons to raise, a fourth child on
the way, and she had recently buried a two-year-old.

William, with the couple's oldest son, left England
without Dorothy. But while he was delayed at the Isle
of Wight trying to find a ship to take him to India, she
delivered her child and had a change of heart. She would
go with her husband, provided her sister accompany the
party.

The dangers Dorothy and her family faced in India
were monumental. The heat was oppressive, and she and
the children were frequently ill with fevers and dysentery.
Daily they encountered wild animals and poisonous snakes.
The worst trial occurred in 1794 when their five-year-old
son died. Soon Dorothy became mentally unstable—and
for the last twenty years of her life, she was confined with
the diagnosis of insanity.

Although Dorothy was little help to her husband in
missionary work, she went— she was willing. Was Dorothy

a failure as a missionary wife? No! She answered yes and
obeyed. That's all God asks of anyone.

ANGELINA GRIMKÉ

Author, Abolitionist (1805–79)

*"Now, Lord, consider their threats and enable your servants
to speak your word with great boldness."*
ACTS 4:29 NIV

Angelina Grimké was raised on a South Carolina plantation by an aristocratic, slaveholding family. A devout
Christian, she accepted slavery as the norm until Sarah, her
sister, traveled to Philadelphia with their father and heard
abolitionists speak against slavery. When Sarah returned,
Angelina became convinced the slave system was wrong,
and she began a Sunday school class for slaves. She also
taught them to read, although it was against the state's law.
When she openly voiced her views of slavery, she was ostra-
cized from family and neighbors. Eventually, she was forced
to join her sister in the North.

In Philadelphia, Angelina made another choice: She
aligned herself with Quaker abolitionists and the Female
Anti-Slavery Society. In 1836, she wrote a pamphlet to
Christian Southern women, calling for them to "overturn a
system of complicated crime." Her writings were publicly
burned in South Carolina, and authorities threatened to
arrest her if she returned to the state.

Angelina spoke to Northern audiences, giving

eyewitness details of slavery, asking women to actively stand against the system. Many people thought she disobeyed New Testament rules for female behavior by speaking and preaching to mixed crowds. Because a female speaker was a rarity, large crowds gathered to hear her, but the meetings were often interrupted by mobs throwing rocks and shattering windows. In 1837, she became the first woman to speak before the Massachusetts State Legislature.

When Angelina married abolitionist Theodore Weld, together they became more aggressive in their fight against the slave system. They wrote *American Slavery as It Is: Testimony of a Thousand Voices*, a story of the horrors slaves faced daily.

After her father's death, Angelina was given her share of the family estate, and she immediately freed the slaves she had inherited. When she discovered her brother had fathered two sons by a slave, she took the boys into her home and sponsored their education.

When confronted with truth, Angelina made biblically based choices, although it meant alienation from family and friends. When she had to choose whether to be quiet or speak against an evil, she spoke boldly. When she had to choose between her Christian convictions or popular opinion, Angelina followed her convictions. Were the choices easy? No, it is never easy to stand with the minority.

Today we face evil in many forms: abortion, child abuse, prostitution, alcoholism, and human trafficking to name a few. We can allow these free rein—or we, like Angelina Grimké, can boldly speak against wrong, choosing what is right and godly.

VONETTE BRIGHT

Founder of the National Day of Prayer (1926–)

*Pray at all times and on every occasion
in the power of the Holy Spirit.
Stay alert and be persistent in your prayers
for all Christians everywhere.*
EPHESIANS 6:18 NLT

Vonette Zachery was a freshman at Texas Women's
University when she received a letter from a hometown
acquaintance, Bill Bright. Flowers and candy followed—
and soon, romance blossomed. Bill attended college in
California, and when Vonette visited him, he realized she
was not a Christian. He asked his friend, Henrietta Mears,
to talk to her, and that day, Vonette became a believer. In
1948, she and Bill were married.

The Brights saw the need for Christian ministries on
college campuses, and Campus Crusade for Christ was
born. The couple organized a twenty-four-hour prayer
chain at their headquarters near the UCLA campus, and
the ministry grew. Vonette said, "We surrounded everything we did with constant prayer."

Convinced that prayer is America's greatest resource,
Vonette founded the National Day of Prayer Task Force
and served as the chairwoman for nine years. In 1988,
she introduced legislation to establish a day of nationwide
prayer. When President Ronald Reagan signed the bill, the
first Thursday of May became America's National Day of
Prayer.

Prayer! A few simple words. God changes hearts and nations when we call on Him in prayer.

CORRIE TEN BOOM

Author, Evangelist (1892–1983)

You have been a refuge for the poor,
a refuge for the needy in his distress,
a shelter from the storm and a shade from the heat.
ISAIAH 25:4 NIV

Corrie ten Boom possibly thought she would live out her days peacefully as a watchmaker in Holland as her father before her. It was not to be. In 1939, as Hitler's armies swept across Europe, he targeted certain people for annihilation, among them the Jews. Corrie's father believed God's people should be protected, and the ten Boom family began hiding the threatened people in their home.

One day in 1944, a man secretly working for the Nazis came to Corrie asking help for his wife, whom he claimed had been arrested for aiding Jews. Corrie quickly gathered the money needed to pay the bribe for the woman's release. In a few minutes, Gestapo agents stormed into the clock shop, arresting Corrie, her father, and thirty-five others.

Within ten days of his arrest, Corrie's eighty-four-year-old father died. Soon she, with her sister Betsie, was imprisoned in a concentration camp. As Allied troops came closer to Holland in 1944, Corrie, with others, was herded into a boxcar, bound for Germany and the dreaded women's extermination camp, Ravensbrück.

One of the first indignities at Ravensbrück was an inspection, which required the women to walk naked before the male guards. Before Corrie stripped off her clothes, she reached into her pillowcase and pulled out a small Bible, which she hid behind a pile of benches. After she showered, Corrie was issued a thin dress and a pair of shoes. She found the Bible and quickly put it in a bag with a cord around her neck. The officers searched the woman ahead of Corrie. Behind her Betsie was searched. No one touched Corrie. As she and Betsie read the Bible to the women in Barracks 8, their building became known as "the crazy place where they have hope."

Food was scarce at Ravensbrück, and treatment was unbelievably cruel with roll call at 4:30 a.m. Yet as Corrie read the Bible, new revelations leaped from the pages. One morning, as the women stood at attention, Corrie leaned ahead and whispered to Betsie, "They took Jesus' clothes, too, and I've never thanked Him for it."

When the prisoners were moved to new barracks, the place swarmed with fleas. There were no individual cots, only huge platforms where the women slept nine across on filthy straw. Betsie reminded her of a scripture they had read that morning: "Giving thanks always for all things" (Ephesians 5:20 KJV). The two thanked God that because the women were closer together, more could hear the scripture readings. They also thanked God for the fleas. Because of them, the guards stayed away from Barracks 28.

During the day, Corrie pushed heavy handcarts to a railroad siding. And each evening women listened as Corrie read from the little Bible. Soon the crowds increased, and they had a second service.

With little food and hard work, Betsie became ill. As she weakened, she saw in a vision a rehabilitation home where those ravaged by war would come to heal. "Corrie, you must tell them," Betsie said. "Your whole life has been training for the work you are doing in prison—and for the work you will do afterwards."

Ninety-six thousand women perished in Ravensbrück. Betsie was one of them. At roll call four days after Betsie's death, Corrie's name was called. *Does this mean the gas chamber?* she wondered. Instead, Corrie was released. A week later, all women her age died in the gas chambers.

Doors opened for Corrie to share her experiences—and over the next thirty years, she preached in sixty-one countries. Everywhere her message was the same: No pit can be so deep that Jesus is not deeper still. No wonder the words JESUS IS VICTOR are engraved on her tombstone.

Through God's Word, Corrie tapped into a well of strength that prison, cruelty, hunger, and death could not conquer. Whatever tragedy we are now experiencing or will in the future, we are not defeated. *Jesus is our victory!*

CARRIE NATION

Activist, Preacher, Author (1846–1911)

Do not join those who drink too much wine
or gorge themselves on meat,
for drunkards and gluttons become poor,
and drowsiness clothes them in rags.
PROVERBS 23:20–21 NIV

As a young woman, Carrie became acquainted with the evils of demon rum when she married a man who became an alcoholic. After his death, she married David Nation, a minister and a lawyer. The couple moved to Medicine Lodge, Kansas, where Carrie again saw the ravages of liquor as she worked as a jail evangelist and led a temperance group.

Carrie and the temperance women took their campaign against alcohol to a new level when they asked saloon keepers if they could hold gospel services on the premises. With Bibles in hand, the women sang and preached to the patrons. Later they grew more aggressive as they broke saloon windows and smashed liquor bottles. In a ten-year span, Carrie was arrested thirty times for disturbing the peace. Yet her efforts proved successful when the saloons in Medicine Lodge closed for a time.

While Carrie Nation's methods were extreme, we admire her courage and sincerity. Her efforts brought to light the problems associated with alcohol. There are many things that, if we succumb to addiction, bring sorrow and strife, impair judgment, and lead to poverty. A wise person will take the advice of scripture and follow a path of sober reflection and wholesome living.

DALE EVANS ROGERS

Actress, Singer, Author (1912–2001)

"Here on earth you will have many trials and sorrows. But take heart, because I have overcome the world."
JOHN 16:33 NLT

In 1947, when Dale Evans, the Queen of the West, married Roy Rogers, the King of the Cowboys, she wondered if their marriage would stand the pressures of a Hollywood lifestyle.

Dale, a native of Texas, had asked Jesus into her life at age ten. She married at fourteen and had a son by age fifteen. The couple soon divorced. Dale's second marriage also failed.

She moved to California, did a screen test, and met Roy Rogers. When his wife died, leaving him with three small children, Roy asked Dale to marry him. Dale worried that his children would not accept her as a new mother. But Dale's son, Tom, suggested the solution might be as close as the nearest church.

She took her son's advice—and the first Sunday Dale walked into a church, the pastor's sermon title was "The House That Is Built on the Rock." Soon the Rogers's children were attending Sunday school, saying grace before meals, having family devotions, and memorizing Bible verses.

In 1950, the world rejoiced when Dale announced she was pregnant. When Robin Elizabeth was born, she was diagnosed with Down syndrome. In the next years, the family grew closer as they coped with Robin's numerous health problems. At age two, Robin died. Dale wrote her story, *Angel Unaware*, to encourage parents who had lost a child.

Two years later, Dale and Roy adopted baby Dodie and six-year-old Sandy, an abused child. Soon Mimi, a child from Scotland, and Debbie Lee, a part-Korean, part–Puerto Rican girl, joined the family.

Yet sorrow was never far from Dale and Roy. When Debbie Lee was twelve, she went on a church trip. A tire on the bus blew, the driver lost control, and Debbie Lee was thrown through a window and died. Dale wrote *Dearest Debbie* in her memory.

It had been Sandy's dream to join the army—and, in spite of handicaps, he passed the physical examination. Stationed in Germany, Sandy was encouraged by fellow soldiers to drink liquor. One night, he overdosed. Again Dale, with her family, made the sad trip to Forest Lawn Cemetery. Dale wrote a tribute to their son, *Salute to Sandy*. To further honor his memory, Dale and Roy traveled to Vietnam to entertain servicemen.

With her faith firm in Christ, Dale Evans triumphed over the almost insurmountable sorrow of losing three children. Because Jesus overcame death, those who trust in Him will also find strength to rise from sorrow's ashes to His peace and hope.

BETTY ANN OLSON

Missionary Martyr (1934–67)

My help comes from the LORD,
who made the heavens and the earth!
PSALM 121:2 NLT

When Betty Ann Olson was seventeen, her missionary mother died—and the once-loving child turned into a defiant young woman. After training as a nurse, Betty wanted to use her skills on the foreign field, but no mission board would accept her. She went to Africa to help her missionary father and stepmother, but she caused so many problems, they asked her to leave.

Betty returned to the United States, and after receiving Christian counseling, she turned her life around and was accepted for mission work in Vietnam. In 1968, the Viet Cong attacked the mission, taking Betty and fellow missionary Henry Blood hostage. Also captured was Mike Benge, an American journalist.

Chained together, the three were marched through the jungle. Food was scarce and mistreatment was common. Betty, weakened by dysentery and fevers, was kicked and dragged by the Viet Cong soldiers to make her move. She died on September 28, 1967. Mike survived and said, "She never showed any bitterness or resentment. To the end, she loved the ones who mistreated her."

Beset by anger and rebellion as a young person, when Betty sought help, her life changed. No one is too far gone. No one is beyond God's help. There is *always* hope and help for every person in God.

ELIZABETH BLACKWELL

First Female Physician in the United States
(1821–1910)

"I command you—be strong and courageous!
Do not be afraid or discouraged.
For the LORD your God is with you wherever you go."
JOSHUA 1:9 NLT

Imagine the stir at Geneva (New York) College of Medicine
in 1847 when Elizabeth Blackwell appeared in class one
day. At that time, it was considered improper for women
to study the human body, the medical profession being for
men only.

Elizabeth was born in England and came to America
with her family in 1832. Her father, a businessman and
staunch abolitionist, was also a lay minister. The family
read the Bible, prayed together, and faithfully attended
church.

When Elizabeth's father died, leaving the family penniless, she became a teacher. But she didn't like teaching
and considered other ways to make a living. Yet there were
few career options for women in that era. An ill friend suggested Elizabeth consider the medical field. After much
thought, Elizabeth said, "I have made up my mind to
devote myself to the study of medicine." She planned to
become a surgeon.

Elizabeth applied to twenty-eight medical schools.
School administrators ridiculed her application. Others
laughed at the idea of a woman becoming a doctor. Each

school informed her they did not admit women.

Because Elizabeth had no income, she also faced the problem of tuition. She taught school and saved her money. When she was not teaching, she studied medical books. Eventually Elizabeth moved to Philadelphia where she hoped to attend one of the city's four medical schools. Finally, she asked a famous doctor, Joseph Warrington, to use his influence to help. He wrote a letter to Geneva Medical College, and they decided to admit her if the 129 male students agreed. Thinking it was a joke, the men voted in favor.

Elizabeth braved prejudice from professors and students. She once told an instructor that if her presence was upsetting, she'd be happy to remove her bonnet and sit in the rear of the classroom. When a professor was to lecture on male anatomy, he asked her not to attend class. Elizabeth told him the human body was holy, and she would not miss the lecture. When she walked into class the next day, the students cheered. In time, teachers and male students began treating her like a sister.

In January of 1849, Elizabeth graduated with honors to become the first woman in the United States to earn a medical degree.

Because she was banned from practicing in most American hospitals, friends advised her to go to Paris. Even in Europe, however, she met with opposition to women physicians—and one doctor suggested she disguise herself as a man. While in France, Elizabeth trained to treat women in childbirth. There she contracted an eye infection that resulted in the removal of one eye, which forced her to give up her dream of becoming a surgeon. During a visit to England, she became friends with young Florence Nightingale, whom Elizabeth encouraged to pursue a career in nursing.

She returned to America and planned to open an office in New York, but no one would rent her space. Elizabeth finally obtained a room in a church basement where she lectured on health and sanitation. Eventually, she obtained a small office in the slums and treated poor women and children.

Emily, her sister, had also graduated from medical school—and, together with another female doctor, they founded New York Infirmary, a small hospital for women and children.

During the Civil War, Elizabeth recruited and trained nurses for the Union Army. In 1868, she established Women's Medical College where she trained other women to become doctors.

Elizabeth Blackwell bravely walked where no woman had ever walked, paving the way for women to become physicians. No doubt it was a painful, lonely path. When we stand for what is right, we may also meet with scorn and rejection. However, when our cause is just, God will help us—and we will reach our goals using our God-given talents.

LADY JANE GREY

English Queen, Martyr (1537–54)

We are therefore Christ's ambassadors,
as though God were making his appeal through us.
2 CORINTHIANS 5:20 NIV

Under the tutelage of Mr. Aylmer, English aristocrat Lady Jane Grey became proficient in Latin, Greek, Italian, and French. She was also a strong Christian, speaking boldly for Christ.

When King Edward VI was near death, he gave Lady Jane the right to succeed him as England's ruler. However, the throne rightfully belonged to his sister, Mary, a Catholic. Lady Jane, too, recognized Mary as the heir—but being young, she had little to say in the decision. Nine days after Lady Jane was crowned, Mary proclaimed herself queen.

Lady Jane was charged with treason—and she, her husband, and parents were imprisoned and condemned to die. When Lady Jane was taken to her execution, she gave a bold testimony for Christ that moved onlookers to tears. Before she was beheaded, she recited Psalm 51. As her head lay on the chopping block, she said, "Lord, into thy hand I commend my spirit."

It is not difficult to speak for Jesus when conditions are ideal. It is quite another matter when our lives are in danger. Lady Jane calmly, consistently, gave her testimony up to the end of her short life. May we also be so convinced of our Savior's cause that we speak boldly as His ambassadors in life and in death.

GERTRUDE CHAMBERS

Author (1883–1966)

Your attitude should be the same as that of Christ Jesus. . .
he humbled himself and became obedient
to death—even death on a cross!
PHILIPPIANS 2:5–8 NIV

Oswald Chambers would have been known as a great Bible
teacher—however, without his wife, his writings could
have been forever lost to succeeding generations. Because
of Biddy, as Oswald called her, the devotional book *My
Utmost for His Highest* has been in print continuously
since 1935, and currently is available in forty languages.
It remains in the top ten titles of religious book bestsellers
with millions of copies in print. Next to the Bible, it is the
most used devotional book and is considered a Christian
classic.

Gertrude Hobbs was sickly as a child, suffering from
chronic bouts of bronchitis. So her older brother and sister
could continue their education, Gertrude left school to
help their mother at home. Eventually, she learned Pitman
shorthand, studying and practicing so that by the time she
was old enough to work full-time, she could take dictation
at a rate of 250 words per minute.

In 1908, Gertrude sailed to the United States where
she met Oswald Chambers, a Scottish Bible scholar,
who traveled the world conducting Bible conferences.
They married in 1910. Oswald had founded the Bible
Training College in London, and this became the couple's

first home. There Biddy began taking shorthand notes of her husband's lectures, as well as opening their home to missionaries and others who needed a place to rest and recuperate.

With the onset of World War I, Oswald offered his services as a YMCA chaplain to the troops. In 1915, the couple and their young daughter sailed to Egypt to minister to British, Australian, and New Zealand soldiers. While Oswald taught the Bible to the men, Biddy busily recorded his sermon notes in shorthand and once again offered the hospitality of their home to those who needed it.

In 1917, Oswald became ill with appendicitis and underwent surgery. He developed complications and died at age forty-three. He and Biddy had been married only seven years.

Biddy, a destitute thirty-four-year-old widow with a small child, returned to London where she operated a busy boardinghouse. Would her husband's voice be forever silenced? Biddy determined this would not happen. She contacted an editor who showed an interest in her notes of Oswald's teachings.

Biddy, although busy with duties as a landlady and mother, undertook the tremendous task of transcribing hundreds of shorthand notes of his sermons into a 365-day devotional book, each with one theme. After three years of work, *My Utmost for His Highest* appeared in print. Nowhere in the book does Biddy mention her part in the publication. In the book's foreword, the letters "B.C." appear.

Oswald Chambers wrote only one book—but today, because of Biddy's untiring efforts, more than thirty titles bear his name. Biddy Chambers well deserves the title of humble servant of God.

Our human nature craves recognition, but Jesus taught that His disciples willingly, humbly serve unnoticed behind the scenes. This was the attitude of the lowly carpenter from Nazareth, and He desires the same of His followers.

ANNE BRADSTREET

First Notable American Female Poet (1612–72)

Let us encourage one another—
and all the more as you see the Day approaching.
HEBREWS 10:25 NIV

Life was hard for the Puritans who came to the Massachusetts Bay Colony in 1630. It had been especially difficult for Anne Bradstreet to leave England, where her father had worked for a nobleman. There, she had lived in a manor house in which she had access to a vast library and neatly manicured gardens. Now she and her family were thrust into a raw, harsh world.

In America, Anne birthed eight children, and with other colonists, struggled to survive. But in the midst of child-rearing problems and household chores, Anne stole away to write poetry. In 1647, her brother-in-law sailed for England and, unknown to Anne, he took her writings with him and had them published. Her book of poems *The Tenth Muse Lately Sprung Up in America*, recording the struggles of a Christian, was well received in England. A second book, *Religious Experiences*, was read by people on both sides of the Atlantic and encouraged those who, like Anne, questioned the meaning of life.

As we come closer to Christ's return, we will face difficult days. Even now, people around us are suffering various degrees of discouragement. Cultivate the habit of speaking encouraging words to everyone. It may be the only glimmer of light on some friend's pathway.

RUTH BELL GRAHAM

Housewife, Mother, Author (1920–2007)

*"My thoughts are completely different
from yours," says the LORD.
"And my ways are far beyond anything you could imagine."*
ISAIAH 55:8 NLT

As a young person, Ruth Bell thought she knew God's plan for her life: She would be a single missionary to Tibet. Born in China to missionary parents, her father was a doctor, her mother a nurse. Although it was a time of political unrest in the country, Ruth never remembers her parents being afraid.

At that time, missionary parents sent their children to boarding schools—and the Bells sent thirteen-year-old Ruth and her older sister to a school in North Korea. When Ruth became homesick, she turned to the Bible for comfort.

While her parents remained in China, Ruth—at eighteen—came to the United States to attend Wheaton

College. Her focus for the future was Tibet.

Ruth accepted the Christian faith as passed to her from loving parents, but at college, for the first time she had doubts about God and the Bible. *Who is Jesus?* she asked herself. She finally came to the realization that some questions of faith cannot be answered. Believers simply accept God and His Word. With that knowledge, she experienced a deepening of her faith.

At college Ruth met Billy Graham. He, too, knew his life work: He would be a preacher. Ruth's first contact with Billy was when she heard him pray. She had never heard anyone pray that way, and she sensed that here was a man who had a special relationship with God.

On the couple's first date, they attended a performance of Handel's *Messiah*. When Ruth returned to her room that night, she fell to her knees and prayed, "If you let me serve You with that man, I would consider it the greatest privilege of my life."

Ruth felt drawn to the young man from North Carolina—and because she was going to Tibet, she encouraged Billy to also consider a missionary calling. About that time, Tibet closed to missionary efforts and Billy Graham proposed to Ruth. They married in 1943.

For a year, Billy served as a pastor in a church in Illinois—but soon an opportunity came for him to work with Youth for Christ. This led to evangelistic meetings, which meant the couple would be separated for weeks.

At first Ruth became ill when her husband left home. But as it became evident Billy's calling was evangelism, Ruth came to grips with the separations. Soul-winning— Billy's passion—now was also hers.

With the arrival of children—five in all—Ruth kept busy with their care. She had her own revival at home as she spent hours studying the Bible and paged through magazines and books looking for sermon illustrations for Billy. She also worked in her local Presbyterian church where she had a ministry to college students.

During the Los Angeles tent crusade in 1949, Ruth left the children with family members to attend the meetings. A notorious criminal, Jim Vaus, was converted in the crusade, along with radio star Stuart Hamblen. When their conversion stories were reported in newspapers across America, Billy Graham became nationally known. Now Ruth was even more convinced that evangelism was her husband's calling—hers was to stay home and care for their children.

As Billy would be away from home for up to six months at a time, Ruth learned that the call to motherhood was hard work. If an appliance needed repairs, she took care of it. When child-rearing problems arose, she dealt with the situation. While her job wasn't as glamorous as that of a missionary, or being at the side of a successful evangelist, Ruth was happy in her calling as mother and wife.

While she worried the children would suffer from their father's absence, she had confidence that God would make up the slack. For several years, Ruth's parents lived nearby and Dr. Bell was a father figure to the Graham children.

Ruth Graham's mission field was not Tibet. Through her husband—and eventually their children—it became the world. When we pray for God's will, we should not be surprised when some doors close while others swing open.

ELIZABETH PAYSON PRENTISS

Hymn Writer, Author (1818–78)

In thy presence is fulness of joy;
at thy right hand there are pleasures for evermore.
PSALM 16:11 KJV

In spite of personal tragedy and poor health most of her life, Elizabeth Prentiss found great joy in her Christian walk. She wrote: "You can't think how sweet it is to be a pastor's wife. . .to sympathize with those who mourn. . .to keep testifying to them what Christ can and will become to them."

Elizabeth experienced painful losses when her four-year-old child and a newborn died within three months. She eventually had three healthy children and went on to write the *Little Suzy* series for children. Her most famous book is a Christian novel, *Stepping Heavenward.*

Elizabeth is most remembered for her hymn, "More Love to Thee, O Christ," which opens a window into a heart of deep devotion to Jesus.

More love to Thee, O Christ, more love to Thee!
Hear Thou the prayer I make on bended knee.
This is my earnest plea: More love, O Christ to Thee,
More love to Thee, more love to Thee!

Jesus intends for believers to find great joy in serving Him—but often, present heartaches cloud our happiness. Yet, like Elizabeth Prentiss, it is possible for us to look higher than the immediate into the face of our loving Savior—and rejoice!

FRANCES WILLARD

Reformer, Teacher, Author (1839–98)

"Choose today whom you will serve. Would you prefer the gods your ancestors served beyond the Euphrates? . . . But as for me and my family, we will serve the LORD."
JOSHUA 24:15 NLT

While twenty to thirty women knelt in the snow in front of a Chicago saloon, the barkeeper stood nearby wringing his hands. The praying, hymn-singing women had already closed fifteen saloons that week by their aggressive actions. A crowd gathered, and a woman began to pray for the men whose lives "demon liquor" had ruined. The woman was Frances Willard.

Alcohol consumption was a serious problem in the United States following the Civil War. Money that should have been used to feed and clothe children went to saloon keepers. As mothers saw their families suffer, they demanded the sale of liquor be prohibited. In 1873, they banded together to pray and formed the Women's Christian Temperance Union. Frances Willard became president of the national WCTU in 1879.

Frances was born on a farm in Wisconsin. Although her parents were Christians, as a young person, she questioned if the Bible was true. She doubted the existence of God. When Frances attended Northwestern Female College in Illinois, she voiced her radical views, and the college president called for special prayer for the student whom he labeled an "infidel."

That summer, Frances became sick with typhoid fever. As she struggled with the disease, she said two voices spoke to her. One encouraged her to commit her life to Christ. The other told her not to give in to such weakness. She obeyed the first voice.

Frances taught school for fifteen years. She spent two years in Europe. In 1871, she became president of Evanston College for Ladies. For a time, she worked with evangelist D. L. Moody.

When Frances was offered the position of national president of the WCTU, she was uncertain as to God's will. After praying about her decision, she opened her Bible to Psalm 37:3 (KJV): "Trust in the LORD, and do good; so shalt thou dwell in the land, and verily thou shalt be fed." She accepted the position without pay.

Under her leadership, the membership of the WCTU reached half a million and became the largest nineteenth-century women's organization in the United States. Soon Frances Willard was a recognized name across America.

As a young woman, Frances chose to follow Christ—and all her future activities were filtered through her deep religious faith. Our choices are important. As we choose the good and right, these choices will also have a positive influence on our families, churches, communities, even the entire world.

CECIL FRANCES ALEXANDER

Hymn Writer (1818–96)

*"I tell you the truth, anyone who will not receive the kingdom
of God like a little child will never enter it."
And he took the children in his arms,
put his hands on them and blessed them.*
MARK 10:15–16 NIV

Although Cecil Alexander was a busy pastor's wife in
Ireland, she took time for children and taught them about
God through her poems and songs. When she published
a hymnbook, she gave the profits to help handicapped
children. Her hymn "There Is a Green Hill Far Away" has
been described as a near-perfect hymn and was intended
to teach children God's plan of salvation. Cecil wrote more
than four hundred songs and poems in which she explained
Jesus' love to children.

Cecil began writing poetry at age nine. Fearing her
father would not approve, she hid her writings under a bedroom rug. When her father found the poems, he gave Cecil
a box to store them in—and on Saturday evenings, he read
his daughter's poems to the family.

Children believe what they are told. They realize their
helplessness and readily turn to another for help. Adults
would do well to come to God in the same way. In fact, possessing the faith of a child *is* our entrance into His kingdom.

FLORENCE NIGHTINGALE

Nurse, Social Reformer (1820–1910)

*A vast crowd was there as he stepped from the boat,
and he had compassion on them and healed their sick.*
MATTHEW 14:14 NLT

Florence Nightingale's father, a banker, taught her Latin, German, French, and Italian. He also instructed her in Greek so she could read the New Testament in the original language. Florence's mother, a socialite, favored elegant parties, travel, and being waited on by servants. From this aristocratic union emerged a daughter, who, at an early age, rejected an affluent lifestyle, showing compassion for sick people and animals.

At age seventeen, Florence said God spoke to her and called her into His service. When she announced to her family her intention to train as a nurse, they reacted with horror. Nursing at that time was an occupation reserved for drunkards and prostitutes. To be admitted to a hospital in that era was a death sentence.

Traveling in Europe with her parents and sister, young Florence said, "I craved some occupation, for something worth doing, instead of frittering time away on useless trifles." At age thirty-two, she persuaded her parents to allow her to attend the Institute of Protestant Deaconesses at Kaiserswerth in Germany where she observed the compassionate care of former women convicts and the insane. She compared the happy lives of the deaconesses to those of her wealthy friends, who complained they "go mad for want of something to do."

Florence returned to England and again begged her family to allow her to follow her calling. When they gave their assent, she became superintendent of a women's hospital and took steps to change the dismal conditions of England's hospitals.

In 1854, Florence heard of the appalling conditions of wounded soldiers in the Crimea during England's war with Russia. Forty-one percent of the men died from wounds and diseases. Thirty-eight nurses volunteered to accompany Florence to the war zone. Upon entering the massive gates of the hospital in Scutari, Florence said, "Abandon hope, all ye who enter here." The hospital was overrun by rats and fleas. Cholera and dysentery killed more men than the enemy. The food was not edible. The wounded lay on the floor without water, bandages, or medicine.

Florence, a brilliant administrator, set up a nursing schedule. She opened kitchens that offered special diets. She wrote countless letters begging for supplies.

Upon the nurses' arrival, there were six hundred wounded at the hospital—but as the war continued, the census rose to three thousand. As Florence and the nurses worked to change conditions for the wounded, they were opposed by officers and doctors who didn't want a female dictating to them. When the British press reported the changes brought by the nurses, opposition subsided.

With kindness and respect, Florence cared for the wounded, and the men saw compassion in action. They called it "Nightingale power." No job was beneath her. Besides her administrative duties, she scrubbed floors, and at night, she could be seen passing between the cots with a light in her hand. One observer said, "I much admired her manner. . . . It was so tender and kind." Soldiers compared the hospital to a church, and Florence, the minister. With improved conditions, the hospital death rate dropped to less than three percent.

Single-handedly, Florence Nightingale transformed public opinion of two professions. Before the Crimean War, British army officers regarded their men as no better than animals. Because of her compassionate treatment of soldiers, officers began treating their men with respect. Florence said of nursing, "Christ is the author of our profession." And nursing, too, became an honorable profession.

Florence arrived home from the Crimea a national hero. Gifts flowed in, which she used to found the Nightingale Home for Nurses at St. Thomas's Hospital. Queen Victoria honored her with a cross of diamonds.

Florence continued to work for army reform and improved hospital care. In 1859, she wrote *Notes on Nursing*, a classic book of the profession.

Filled with Christ's compassion, Florence Nightingale gave herself to her calling. Whatever our profession, as we allow Christ's love to fill our hearts, respect, kindness, and blessings will flow from our lives to all we attempt to help. The Christ of Calvary has an abundance of compassion to share with us.

PHOEBE PALMER

Evangelist, Author (1807–74)

*Let us purify ourselves from everything
that contaminates body and spirit,
perfecting holiness out of reverence for God.*
2 CORINTHIANS 7:1 NIV

Early in her life, Phoebe Palmer became convinced that a holy God desires His people to live holy lives. In 1837, she laid claim to an experience of holiness. To help other women reach this goal, she began meetings called the Tuesday Meeting for the Promotion of Holiness. This was the beginning of the "holiness movement" in America and Britain when Christians of every denomination were stirred to seek God to become more like Christ.

Besides raising a family, Phoebe distributed tracts in New York City slums, did prison visitation, and founded Five Points Mission. Later, as her husband traveled in evangelistic meetings, Phoebe served as the "exhorter." Soon, great crowds in America and England came to hear the eloquent woman preacher proclaim the message of holiness. Phoebe's books, *The Way of Holiness* and *Guide to Holiness*, were read widely, and from these roots emerged several holiness denominations.

This "Mother of the Holiness Movement" never sought to be ordained as a minister, yet it is estimated that twenty-five thousand people came to Christ through her preaching.

One day when we see Jesus, we will be like Him (see 1 John 3:2). But until that time, we are admonished to pursue holiness, becoming more like the holy Son of God.

MARIAN ANDERSON

Musician (1897–1993)

The Lord's servant must not quarrel; instead,
he must be kind to everyone,
able to teach, not resentful.
Those who oppose him he must gently instruct.
2 TIMOTHY 2:24–25 NIV

When the prestigious conductor Arturo Toscanni heard Marian Anderson sing, he said, "Yours is a voice such as one hears once in a hundred years." But Marian, a black woman, had much to overcome to use her talent.

Marian was born into a poor but loving family in Philadelphia. At age six she began singing in her church choir. Other churches heard of her talent and invited her to sing in their churches. When her father died, money was scarce, and her choir raised money for her first voice lessons. Later, when Marian attempted to enroll at a music academy, she was turned away because of her race. Her mother didn't make a fuss of the incident and assured Marian, "Something will work out."

Marian continued to study voice and perform. But when she gave a recital in New York's Town Hall, the attendance was poor and critics had little good to say about her voice. Discouraged, Marian wondered if she should continue to sing.

Her career again gained momentum when she entered a voice contest and won over more than three hundred rivals. Marian continued to hold concerts in the United States. In

1933 and 1934, she performed 142 concerts in Scandinavia and received rave reviews.

Returning to the United States, she again confronted racism. She received the key to Atlantic City, New Jersey, but was refused a hotel room. She was barred from eating in "whites only" restaurants. In 1939, her manager attempted to rent Constitutional Hall in Washington, D.C., for a concert. "No Negro will ever appear in this hall!" he was told. Many people became outraged, including First Lady Eleanor Roosevelt. Instead, a concert was held on the steps of the Lincoln Memorial on Easter Sunday. That day Marian sang Negro spirituals and operatic arias to seventy-five thousand people while millions more listened by radio.

Marian sang at Dwight Eisenhower's and John F. Kennedy's presidential inaugurations. President Ronald Reagan presented her with the National Medal of Arts. Quietly, Marian faced intolerance and prejudice. She said, "If I were inclined to be combative, I suppose I might insist on making an issue of these things. But. . .my mission is to leave behind me the kind of impression that will make it easier for those who follow." Following her mother's advice and the admonition of scripture, Marian fought prejudice with gentleness.

Little is accomplished when we attack prejudice with angry words. We fight intolerance more effectively following our Lord's example—with quietness and kindness.

JANET PARSHALL

Broadcaster, Author (1950–)

I heard the Lord asking,
"Whom should I send as a messenger to my people?
Who will go for us?" And I said, "Lord, I'll go! Send me."
ISAIAH 6:8 NLT

As a young Christian, Janet Parshall thought God wanted her to serve on the foreign mission field. She received a degree in music, married, and had four children. As a stay-at-home mother, Janet was aware of world events that threatened her children's future.

She wanted to hide from the threats, yet she realized Christians do not run from problems; they confront them. With missionary zeal, using a microphone, Janet did just that. She took a job at a local radio station as a talk show host, commenting on world issues, interviewing guests, and taking listeners' comments. *Janet Parshall's America* is now heard on eighty stations. She discusses issues affecting the family, such as homosexuality, pornography, abortion, and civil rights.

A concern close to Janet's heart is biblical illiteracy. She believes the American family will only be strong as they know what God says on issues and strive to implement His Word into their lives.

Janet Parshall answered God's plea to "go"—she is involved. The next move is up to each believer. Will we only talk about what's wrong with the world? Or, like Janet, will we go and be salt and light in our homes, churches, and communities?

FANNY CROSBY

Hymn Writer (1820–1915)

*Out of the most severe trial, their overflowing joy
and their extreme poverty welled up in rich generosity.*
2 Corinthians 8:2 NIV

At six months of age, Fanny Crosby contracted a purulent
eye infection. When a doctor treated the condition with
hot poultices, the result was total blindness. The same year,
Fanny's father died and her mother was forced to work outside the home.

In spite of a distressing disability, young Fanny possessed
a cheerful disposition and accepted her blindness. At age
eight she wrote:

> *Oh, what a happy child I am,*
> *Although I cannot see!*
> *I am resolved that in this world*
> *Contented I will be!*

Fanny's grandmother, Eunice, became the little girl's
eyes. The older woman described to Fanny the world
around her until she recognized the call of birds and knew
the color of flowers and the beauty of a sunset. The grandmother and Mrs. Hawley, a landlady, taught Fanny the
Bible until she could recite from memory the Pentateuch,
the Gospels, Proverbs, the Song of Solomon, and many
psalms. Later she would use this knowledge when she wrote
hymns.

Fanny received a good education at the New York Institute for the Blind, and later she taught at the school. She married a blind musician, Alexander van Alstine.

At age thirty, Fanny attended a revival meeting and felt God tug at her heart. She prayed, "Include me! Do not pass me by, Lord." That day she dedicated her life to God and from the experience wrote the invitation hymn "Pass Me Not, O Gentle Savior." Shortly afterward, in a vision, God told her He had a work for her. In 1864, she met William B. Bradbury, a Christian music publisher. When he shared a melody with her, Fanny wrote words for the tune, and from then on her verses took on spiritual meaning.

In the 1860s, Fanny contracted with a publishing company to write three hymns a week, but more often she wrote seven songs a day. For these, she was paid one or two dollars apiece—and the composer of the music usually kept the rights for the hymns. In spite of her success as a hymn writer, Fanny had her critics. One evaluator claimed her poems did not possess high poetic quality. Fanny agreed with them. She said she wanted common, ordinary people to understand her hymns.

One day Fanny needed a specific amount of money and asked God to supply the need. Soon the doorbell rang and a stranger greeted Fanny. As the person left, Fanny felt a bill slip into her hand. It was the exact amount of money she had prayed for. From this experience, she wrote the hymn "All the Way My Savior Leads Me."

Most of Fanny's hymns were written in the first ten years of her hymn-writing ministry. When she was over sixty, she began spending several days a week speaking and counseling at New York City missions. She said of the alcoholics, prostitutes, and jobless she encountered, "You can't save a man by telling him of his sins. Tell him there is pardon and love waiting him." She wrote the hymn "Rescue the Perishing" to encourage believers to reach out in love to destitute people.

Fanny never wasted time feeling sorry for herself. When evangelist D. L. Moody asked her if she had one wish, what it would be, he thought she'd ask for her sight. Instead, Fanny said, "I'd wish that I might continue blind the rest of my life."

In her nineties, Fanny, described as extremely thin and bent over nearly double, said of her life, "I am so busy I hardly know my name." This blind woman seemed destined for obscurity. Yet during her lifetime, she became acquainted with four United States presidents; addressed the U.S. Congress on the needs of the blind; wrote more than seven thousand hymns; and, at age ninety-three, spoke in Carnegie Hall. By her life and with her hymns, she has blessed people in all walks of life.

Our human nature is prone to dwell on what we lack. As we follow Fanny Crosby's spirited example, we will take the jewel of joyfulness and move on to the wonders of God's plans for our lives.

BETH MOORE

Bible Teacher, Author (1957–)

For the word of God is full of living power.
It is sharper than the sharpest knife,
cutting deep into our innermost thoughts and desires.
HEBREWS 4:12 NLT

As a child growing up in Arkansas, Beth Moore loved listening to the stories she heard about Jesus in her church. In her teen years, Beth sensed God had a work for her to do; and although she didn't know what it would be, she said yes.

After college, marriage, and the birth of two daughters, Beth began teaching a Sunday school class. As she studied the scriptures, she felt her lack of biblical knowledge. In a Bible doctrine class, she developed a love for the Word of God—and soon Beth was teaching a women's Bible class that grew to include two thousand women.

In 1994, Beth founded Living Proof Ministries, an organization to teach women to love and live by God's Word. The organization expanded, and now Beth's Bible study books are distributed worldwide. Living Proof Live conferences give Beth the opportunity to encourage women of every race and country to diligently study the Word of God.

As we pick up our Bibles, search its pages, and read it prayerfully, we hold in our hands all we need to solve our problems, heal our hurts, and bring peace to our often confused lives.

KATHRYN KUHLMAN

Evangelist, Author (1907–76)

God chose the foolish things of the world to shame the wise. . .
so that no one may boast before him.
1 CORINTHIANS 1:27, 29 NIV

Skeptics came with their doubts. Scoffers came to ridicule.
The sick came in wheelchairs and on stretchers expecting
healing, and loyal followers came to be blessed. Throngs of
people came to hear "faith healer" Kathryn Kuhlman. And
her audiences were not disappointed as the tall, red-haired
woman in a flowing white dress stood behind the pulpit
and declared, "I believe in miracles!"

One Sunday, as fourteen-year-old Kathryn stood in the
morning service at the Methodist church in her hometown
of Concordia, Missouri, she began trembling until she
could no longer hold the hymnbook. She slipped to the
front pew and, weeping, acknowledged she was a sinner.
Later she said of that time, "In that moment, the blood of
Jesus Christ, God's Son, cleansed me from all sin." God's
Holy Spirit had touched Kathryn, and her life was never the
same.

Kathryn quit high school before her junior year to travel
with an evangelistic team. Then at twenty-one, without
formal training, she went on her own, holding services in
tents and small churches in Idaho. An unlikely candidate
for a speaking ministry, Kathryn had stuttered as a child.
Her mother had encouraged her to talk slowly, and Kathryn
developed the habit of speaking very distinctly. Yet she

didn't want to be known as a preacher or evangelist. All her life she said, "I can't preach." Rather, she claimed to simply "carry a water bucket for the Lord."

In 1933, Kathryn began a church and a radio ministry in Denver. Because of personal problems, this was a difficult time that led her to make a fresh surrender of her life to God. With Kathryn's new dedication, the miracles began.

Later she moved to Franklin, Pennsylvania. One day, while Kathryn was speaking on the resurrection power of Christ, a woman in the audience was healed and a doctor later confirmed the healing. Next, a man blind for twenty-two years received his sight, and the word spread.

Kathryn wrote the book *I Believe in Miracles*, yet she denied being a faith healer. She explained the healing miracles as "just the mercy of God." With the advent of a weekly television program, her followers numbered in the thousands.

Kathryn's faith was simple. She said, "God said it, I believe it, that settles it." She acknowledged God as her source—she was only carrying "the bucket" from which He dispensed His blessings. As we accomplish feats large or small for our Lord, we do well to also humbly give Him all the glory.

TWILA PARIS

Composer, Vocalist, Author (1958–)

Worship the LORD with gladness;
come before him with joyful songs.
PSALM 100:2 NIV

Twila Paris believes a Christian's high calling is to worship God, and she writes music such as "We Bow Down" and "He Is Exalted" to assist believers in doing this. She has released twenty-two albums. Three times, she was named Gospel Music Association Female Vocalist of the Year. Called a modern-day psalmist, Twila's songs can be found in numerous church hymnals. She also coauthored the book *In This Sanctuary*, in which she explains the importance of worship.

Raised in a Christian family, Twila's parents gathered daily their four children for family worship. They were also a musical family who loved the hymns of the church. Twila displayed an interest in music at a young age and began piano lessons when she was six. Her career as a singer-songwriter began in 1981 with the release of her first full-length album, *Knowin' You're Around*.

Where does Twila find inspiration for her music? She says, "God raises the window a crack and slips in a song every now and then. I find worship rises in such a natural way."

Worship to God may be expressed by a simple "thank you" or in a song of joy. Either way, we do well to follow the psalmist's admonition to worship the Lord with a glad heart.

JONI EARECKSON TADA

Advocate for Disabled, Author (1949–)

"Here on earth you will have many trials and sorrows.
But take heart, because I have overcome the world."
JOHN 16:33 NLT

At seventeen, Joni Eareckson enjoyed riding horses, swimming, and playing lacrosse. One July day in 1967, she dove into a shallow spot in Chesapeake Bay and pounded her head into the bay bottom. She would have drowned except for her sister, who pulled Joni out of the water. At the hospital the doctor told her family the grim news: Joni's spinal cord was permanently damaged. She was paralyzed from the shoulders down.

For the next two years, Joni was in and out of hospitals and rehabilitation centers. Friends came to encourage and pray for her. She questioned, *Why did this happen? How could God allow this?* Joni pled with God to heal her—and when it didn't happen, she became severely depressed. She begged friends to slit her wrists or give her pills to kill her.

Raised in a Christian home, Joni had accepted Jesus during her sophomore year of high school. Slowly, ever so slowly, after her accident, it dawned on her that God possibly had a reason for her injury.

When Joni expressed her frustrations to Steve, another teenager, he had no answers. Instead, he opened his Bible and read to her of Jesus' suffering. Steve said she would find the answers to her questions in Christ. Joni began studying the Bible with Steve, and he asked her to speak to his youth group. Joni felt she spoke poorly, so she took a class in public speaking.

Joni learned to write and draw holding a brush or pen in her mouth. One day a family friend visited the Eareckson home and saw her drawings. He organized an exhibit of her work at a Baltimore restaurant. As Joni mingled with the crowd that day, she was approached by a young fireman who had lost both hands in a fire. Bitter and angry, the man told his story to Joni. For a half hour, she shared with him what she had learned through her disability.

In the next years, Joni faced the challenges of plugged catheters and pressure sores that required weeks of bed rest. Aided by friends, Joni learned to deal with the hurdles.

In 1974, Joni appeared with Barbara Walters on the *Today Show.* This led to invitations to speak to churches and clubs. When she wrote *Joni,* the story of her life, letters flooded her Baltimore home. The book has been translated into thirty languages. She wrote a sequel, *A Step Further,* in which she addressed the problems of the disabled. A film was made of her life in which she played herself. She also created a line of greeting cards.

When Joni expressed a desire to drive a car, a doctor told her she would never drive. Yet when she moved to Los Angeles, another doctor encouraged her to drive, and soon she was maneuvering her car on crowded freeways.

In California, Joni met Ken Tada, a teacher and coach. Romance blossomed, and Joni and Ken married in 1982. Ken now serves with his wife in ministry.

Joni began helping other disabled people—and because she understood the problems they faced, in 1979 she created Joni and Friends International Disability Center, a Christian organization to minister to the disabled and their families. The work is now active in twenty European countries. Her ministry Wheels for the World has distributed thousands of wheelchairs to needy disabled people in more than fifty countries. She is the author of thirty books.

Suffering is a mystery not easily fixed. Joni calls her disability "a severe mercy." Through it, she found a deeper meaning for her life: She is to help others who, like herself, struggle to make sense of suffering.

Trials and sorrows come in many shapes. For Joni, it was the loss of mobility. For others, it may be a seemingly hopeless situation. The scriptures assure us suffering is part of the fabric of life. However, when Christ died on the cross, He overcame every trial and sorrow. As God helped Joni, so He will help all who call on Him in the midst of the tumult.

AUDREY WETHERELL JOHNSON

Bible Study Organizer (1907–84)

Trust in the LORD with all your heart;
do not depend on your own understanding.
Seek his will in all you do, and he will direct your paths.
PROVERBS 3:5–6 NLT

When China closed to missionary efforts in 1950, forty-three-year-old Audrey Wetherell Johnson, a British citizen, reluctantly left the land of her calling and came to America. *What ministry does God have for me now?* she wondered. God reminded her of His past faithfulness, and her heart filled with peace.

While Audrey rested at a friend's home in California, five women asked her to begin a Bible study on the book of Colossians. Audrey hesitated. *Weren't there plenty of churches in America to teach the Bible?* After praying about the request, she prepared a lesson and taught the women. They invited their friends and the group grew.

Bible Study Fellowship—a nonprofit, international, interdenominational organization—mushroomed across America. Within twenty years of its inception, one hundred thousand people had taken Audrey's five-year course. Mothers requested a children's program, and Children's Christian Training Program was born.

It all happened as one displaced missionary rested in God's faithfulness. When our plans fall apart, we need not panic. As God had a plan for Audrey, we can also trust Him to open new paths for us.

LISA BEAMER

Wife of 9/11 Hero Todd Beamer (1969–)

May the God of hope fill you with all joy and peace. . .
so that you may overflow with hope
by the power of the Holy Spirit.
ROMANS 15:13 NIV

"Let's roll!" were the last words Lisa heard her husband say
on a cell phone before his death on September 11, 2001.
Because she hoped in God, Lisa received courage to go
on without him, raise their two young sons, and—four
months after Todd's death—give birth to their daughter.

Lisa was no stranger to tragedy. When she was fifteen,
her faith was shaken when her father died unexpectedly. A
scripture—Jeremiah 29:11—served to comfort her through
the family's sadness. "I know the plans I have for you,"
declares the LORD, "plans to prosper you. . .to give you
hope and a future" (NIV).

Lisa met Todd Beamer at Wheaton College in Chicago.
On May 14, 1994, they married. Soon Todd accepted a
position with a software company in New Jersey. The
couple planned to build a home and live the American
dream.

Both Christians, Lisa and Todd served in their church,
becoming part of a young couples' group that met to discuss issues of faith and the home. Soon the Beamers had a
son, David. Two years later, Drew joined the family. Lisa
was five months pregnant on September 11.

On September 10, the couple returned from a business

trip to Rome. Todd had a flight to catch the next day and rose early. Lisa was getting ready to run errands when her phone rang and a friend asked, "Do you have your television on?"

As she watched the World Trade Center events unfold, Lisa wondered why Todd didn't call. Then the television flashed news of another crash. This one, Flight 93, was bound for San Francisco, Todd's destination. Lisa knew immediately her husband was on that flight. She cried out to God and felt His peace envelop her. *Todd is in heaven,* she thought.

In the aftermath of her husband's death, Lisa attended a memorial service in Pennsylvania, the site of the crash. She was honored by the United States Congress and appeared on numerous television shows. In an interview with Larry King, he said, "You've given a lot of people a lot of hope."

Hope was what Lisa Beamer held on to after her husband's death: hope for her children's future and hope of heaven where she and the children will again be united with Todd.

We don't know what tomorrow will bring. But even when dark clouds of tragedy arise on our horizon, as Christians, our hearts overflow with hope—imparted by the God of hope.

JOY RIDDERHOF

Founder of Gospel Recordings (1903–84)

Be joyful always; pray continually;
give thanks in all circumstances,
for this is God's will for you in Christ Jesus.
1 THESSALONIANS 5:16–18 NIV

While a student at Columbia Bible School, Joy Ridderhof heard a message on "rejoicing evermore"—and she began the practice of giving thanks in every situation. This principle would serve her well in the years ahead.

In 1930, Joy went as a missionary to Honduras. Soon she found herself struggling with malaria, flu, and smallpox. Yet she continued to rejoice. Broken in health, in 1936, she was forced to leave the mission field.

As she lay in her parents' attic bedroom in Los Angeles, Joy pondered her future. The prospect of returning to Honduras was gone. She had no financial support. As she attempted to rejoice, Joy remembered the gramophone machines that had blared out popular tunes in Honduras. She made a three-and-a-half-minute gospel recording in the Spanish language and sent it to the village she had left.

Other missionaries heard of Joy's recording, and they wanted tapes to share with unreached groups. By 1984, Gospel Recordings had provided a tool whereby people in four thousand languages had heard of Jesus' love.

Loss and illness need not lead to despair. God has provided an open door to escape that fate. *Rejoice evermore!* It's more than good advice—it is God's command to His people.

EDITH SCHAEFFER

Author, Cofounder of L'Abri (1914–)

Continue to love each other with true Christian love.
Don't forget to show hospitality to strangers,
for some who have done this have entertained
angels without realizing it!
HEBREWS 13:1–2 NLT

Can a housewife help bring change to a world indifferent
to Christ and the Bible? More important, will the little she
does make a difference? With a teapot in one hand and a
platter of cakes in the other, a smiling Edith Schaeffer *did*
make a difference and helped influence countless people to
follow Christ.

Edith Seville was born in China to missionary parents.
She attended Beaver College in Pennsylvania where she met
ministerial student Francis Schaeffer. They married in 1935.

In 1947, when Europe was recovering from the devas-
tation of World War II, Francis was commissioned by his
denomination to visit Europe to assess the spiritual health
of the churches. He discovered that European churches and
pastors lacked spiritual vitality. Children were being raised
without a knowledge of the Bible. The mission board asked
Edith and Francis to consider moving to the Continent
to strengthen what remained. The Schaeffers moved to
Switzerland in 1948—and while Francis led children and
young people in informal Bible studies, Edith entertained
their guests in a relaxed atmosphere. Soon people of all ages
were being counseled, taught, and fed around Edith's table.

After a furlough in 1954, the Schaeffers experienced a series of difficulties when Frankie, their three-year-old son, became ill with polio. Then the mission board cut the family's salary. Next Susan, their daughter, was diagnosed with rheumatic fever and ordered on bed rest. With every setback, Edith went to God in prayer.

But the trials didn't end. The local Swiss authorities, unfriendly to the Schaeffers' religious influence, ordered them to leave town. *Is our time in Europe over?* Edith wondered as she prayed. While Francis packed for the move, Edith went to neighboring villages looking for a house to rent.

A real estate agent showed her a home near a bus stop that would be ideal for their ministry, but the property was not for rent—it was for sale. Should they buy the house? The Schaeffers needed to know, and Edith again prayed. If God wanted them to have the property, a thousand dollars needed to come in the mail the next day. The following day at ten in the morning, the postman arrived with a letter in his hand. It contained the money.

The new location—called L'Abri, meaning "shelter" in French—became a sanctuary for people of all races, ages, and backgrounds. Often as many as one hundred people would crowd under the Schaeffers' roof. Famous musicians came with questions. Alcoholics came for counseling. Students came to debate Christianity. For some, L'Abri was their last hope. All came searching for truth—and no subject was off limits as the guests discussed music, art, medicine, and the Bible. Some stayed for a day. Others spent weeks and even months.

During the day, Edith supervised the guests as they

helped with meal preparation, gardening, canning, cleaning, and laundry. In the evening, after Edith's sumptuous dinner, the people gathered around the fireplace or stayed by the table to talk. Edith said, "Life at L'Abri was never, ever easy, but it was always rewarding." As guests sipped tea and munched on Edith's homemade goodies, her hospitality became legendary.

Besides the comfort of her guests, Edith also had other issues to deal with. Three of the Schaeffers' four children suffered from chronic diseases. Then Edith's mother-in-law, a stroke victim, moved in with the family.

L'Abri went on to expand to other locations. When her husband was diagnosed with cancer and received treatment at Mayo Clinic in Rochester, Minnesota, Edith established a center there. The purpose of each location was to communicate Christianity in a relaxed, homelike atmosphere.

While Francis's books deal with theological subjects, some of Edith's book titles are *What Is a Family?* and *The Hidden Art of Homemaking*. In all, she published seventeen books.

Some preach or sing of Jesus' love. Others, like Edith Schaeffer, touch lives by cooking, cleaning, and serving meals. Like Edith Schaeffer, try to find simple acts of hospitality to do every day to show others Jesus' love.

AMANDA SMITH

Evangelist (1837–1915)

God chose things despised by the world,
things counted as nothing at all,
and used them. . .so that no one can ever
boast in the presence of God.
1 CORINTHIANS 1:28–29 NLT

While attending a revival meeting in 1868, Amanda Smith saw in a vision the fiery word, "Go!" and heard a voice say, "Go, preach." She said God touched her "from the crown of my head to the soles of my feet." In spite of long days at a washtub, she began holding revival meetings.

There was not a more unlikely person to preach the gospel than Amanda Smith, a former slave with only three and a half months of education. As a young woman, she had worked as a maid in Pennsylvania, where she was converted in a revival service. When she married, her husband—a soldier in the Union army—never returned from war.

Amanda became an effective evangelist. In 1876, an opportunity came for her to preach in England. Later she was invited to conduct meetings in Scotland, India, and Africa. Besides preaching and singing, she organized women's and men's groups and temperance societies.

Whom does God choose to preach His glorious salvation message? Regardless of race, education, status, or background, God calls those who willingly say yes and reserve for Him any glory that results.

PHILLIS WHEATLEY

African-American Poet (1753–84)

"Don't rejoice just because evil spirits obey you;
rejoice because your names are registered
as citizens of heaven."
LUKE 10:20 NLT

Imagine being kidnapped at age seven and thrust into the
hold of a dirty slave ship. After spending several months at
sea, you stand on the auction block dressed only in a piece
of filthy carpet.

That day in 1761, John and Suzanna Wheatley were
looking for a servant to help in their Boston house. Pity
flooded Suzanna's heart as she saw the dirty child, and she
begged John to buy her. Noticing the child's frail condition,
he shook his head. Suzanna persisted.

The Wheatleys brought the sickly child home and
named her Phillis. Reluctant to place her in the cold slave
quarters, Suzanna made a bed for Phillis in a room with the
Wheatleys' daughter, Mary.

Mary showed her new friend around their home, which
included an extensive library. Although most people of the
time believed slaves weren't capable of being educated, when
Phillis showed an interest in learning, Mary taught her to
read and write. Phillis attended church with the family—
and instead of sitting in the gallery with other slaves, the
Wheatleys had her sit with them. Through the influence
of this pious family, Phillis became a devout Christian.
She studied the Bible. Soon she read Latin and the classics.

Around age thirteen, she began writing verse of literary quality.

In 1765, all Boston was in an uproar when the British government passed the Stamp Act, which levied a heavy tax on the colonists. Phillis also felt the tax was unfair and, without the Wheatleys' knowledge, wrote and sent a poem to King George III in England. In a few months a delegation appeared at the Wheatley home. The men marveled that a slave could write a letter like the one the king had received.

Phillis accompanied the Wheatleys to England in 1773. Unknown to her, a Christian woman had thirty-nine of Phillis's poems published in a book. The black slave became popular in London and was known as the "Sable Muse." She was possibly the first black American to have a book published.

While slavery was a serious evil, Phillis's poems do not question the slave system. Rather, her writings thank God for Christian people who brought her the gospel. Phillis's capture made it possible for her to hear of God's wonderful salvation and prepare for a glorious future in eternity beyond.

While many things of life give us great joy, the greatest is knowing we've accepted Jesus, God's provision for our eternal redemption. How glorious to know our names are recorded on heaven's roster!

LILIAS TROTTER

Missionary to North Africa (1853–1928)

Wait patiently for the LORD. Be brave and courageous.
Yes, wait patiently for the LORD
PSALM 27:14 NLT

As a child in a wealthy English family, Lilias Trotter studied art with the goal of becoming an artist. However, this objective became secondary after she trusted in Christ as her Savior.

Young Lilias shared in the religious fervor that swept across England in the 1870s. When she heard Hannah Whitall Smith preach, the Bible teacher became Lilias's role model. Evangelist D. L. Moody held meetings in London, and as Lilias helped counsel converts, she received a passion to lead people to Christ.

Lilias felt called to bring the gospel to the Muslims, and in 1888 she went to North Africa. Knowing Muslims could not be reached by conventional missionary methods, she used her artistic talents to design attractive tracts for distribution. Beginning with three workers, soon thirty missionaries worked full-time in gospel distribution. Her greatest achievement was the translation of the New Testament into the Algerian dialect. Although there were few converts, Lilias plodded on for thirty-eight years. In letters she often wrote, "Blessed are all they that wait for Him."

Sometimes, no matter how hard we work doing good, we see little progress. In those times, we can prayerfully and patiently wait on God. Who is more trustworthy to wait upon?

KATHARINA LUTHER

Wife of the Reformer (1499–1552)

A worthy wife is her husband's joy and crown.
PROVERBS 12:4 NLT

Who would have thought romance could flourish during the dark days of the Protestant Reformation? Affairs of the heart were possibly the last thing on Martin Luther's mind when he nailed his Ninety-five Theses to the door of the Wittenberg church.

On April 4, 1523, under cover of darkness, twelve nuns from the Nimbschen nunnery climbed out of a window and crept into the back of Leonard Koppe's wagon bound for Wittenberg. One of the nuns—feisty, redheaded Katharina von Bora—had entered a convent school at age five when her mother died. At age sixteen, she took vows of chastity, poverty, and obedience.

A few years earlier, Katharina and the other sisters had heard of the radical teacher Martin Luther. While they continued to chant prayers and embroider, their whispered conversations centered on the monk's audacity to refute the church's sale of indulgences as a means of receiving forgiveness of sins.

One of the women, Magdalena von Staupitz, wrote Luther, saying that some of the nuns wanted out of the nunnery and asked for his help. Luther responded that if the elders in Torgau would plan the escape, he would find homes and husbands for the women.

In the next two years, Luther helped eleven of the

women find husbands. For the twelfth escapee, Katharina von Bora, he was unsuccessful. While working for a wealthy family, she fell in love with Jerome Baumgartner, a student. But he left Wittenberg; and when word reached Katharina that he was engaged, she was heartbroken. Another suitor, Dr. Glatz, showed an interest in the ex-nun, but she spurned his attention. Secretly, she had set her sights on Luther. While Luther encouraged other ex-monks to marry, he never planned to himself. As a hunted heretic, his life was often threatened and could end at any moment.

No one is sure what changed Luther's mind—but on June 13, 1525, Katharina, age twenty-six, and Luther, forty-two, married in a quiet ceremony. News of their marriage rocked the Western world. *Hadn't the ex-nun and monk taken irrevocable vows?* Many openly opposed the union, predicting the marriage would produce the Antichrist. Luther explained that he married to "please his father, tease the pope, and spite the devil."

The Luthers' first home was a forsaken monastery. In spite of critics, Katharina proved capable of handling the problems that beset their marriage. She managed their finances, freeing her husband to teach, preach, and write. Luther suffered from various diseases, and Katharina treated him with herbs, poultices, and massages. She operated a brewery, bought cattle, drove a wagon, and maintained a garden and an orchard. Humorously, Luther said she also sometimes found time to read the Bible.

Often, as many as twenty-five guests gathered around Katharina's table as she took in student boarders, refugees fleeing persecution, four orphans of relatives, and the many guests who came to consult with her famous husband.

Luther recognized his wife's able management and said he wouldn't trade his Katie for France and Venice.

Katharina and Luther had six children. But diseases dealt harshly with the young during the Middle Ages, and the couple was saddened when a daughter died at eight months and another girl at age fourteen.

In 1546, Luther became ill while away from home and died without his beloved Katie at his side. War raged in Germany at that time—and a year after her husband's death, Katharina, with the children, was forced to flee their home. They came back in 1547 to find the farm in ruins. For a time, the penniless widow took in boarders. Then a plague hit Wittenberg, and again Katharina and her family fled. While en route, the horses bolted and Katharina fell from the wagon and received severe bruises. She died three months later.

With industry and love, Katharina Luther enriched her husband's life. God has a plan and role for every woman to fill. We each are called to become all God intended us to be, in our homes, our workplaces, our churches, and our communities.

WILHELMINA

Queen of the Netherlands (1880–1962)

The LORD will guide you continually,
watering your life when you are dry
and keeping you healthy, too.
ISAIAH 58:11 NLT

God guides the affairs of individual lives and nations. No one was more aware of this than Wilhelmina, queen of the Netherlands. When her father, King William III, died, ten-year-old Wilhelmina became queen. Encouraged by a devout mother, the princess trusted in Christ. During her formative years, Wilhelmina sought God's guidance for her life and her nation.

When bombs fell and German tanks rolled across the Netherlands in 1940, Queen Wilhelmina determined to stay with her people. But when the situation threatened her life, the queen escaped to England where she directed Dutch forces in Germany and Japan. During World War II, more than 270,000 of her subjects were killed or died from starvation. Wilhelmina broadcast weekly messages to comfort the survivors and encourage them to resist the German occupation. After the war, Wilhelmina abdicated the throne to Juliana, her daughter.

What does a queen do upon retirement? Wilhelmina felt directed to "bring all men to Christ." She did this through radio broadcasts, personal correspondence, and her book *Lonely, but Not Alone*.

How comforting to know God has a plan for every life!

Each day we, like Wilhelmina, can live securely, our lives guided by the hand of a loving Father.

SHIRLEY DOBSON

Author, Chairwoman of National Day
of Prayer Task Force
(1937–)

"If my people, who are called by my name,
will humble themselves and pray
and seek my face and turn from their wicked ways,
then will I hear from heaven
and will forgive their sin and will heal their land."

2 CHRONICLES 7:14 NIV

Shirley Dobson didn't wake up one morning and suddenly believe God answers prayer. Rather, her journey to be chairwoman of America's National Day of Prayer began in childhood.

When Shirley was a little girl, a Sunday school teacher told the students that God loved them and knew each one by name. Shirley believed the teacher and gave her heart to Jesus. The teacher also taught the children how to pray—and when Shirley's parents divorced, she asked God to give her a new father. Within a year her mother married a Christian man, and Shirley realized God had heard and answered her prayer.

Several years later, Shirley asked God to give her a Christian husband. On the campus of Pasadena State

College, where she was pursuing a degree in education, she met James Dobson, captain of the tennis team, and was impressed by his stand for Christian principles. The couple dated for three years and married in 1960. Again God had answered Shirley's prayer.

When their home was blessed with children, Shirley and her husband taught their daughter and son the importance of prayer through times of family devotions.

In the years to come, Shirley and James were alarmed when they saw many American families being ravaged by divorce and other evils. To counteract society's destructive forces, they established Focus on the Family, an organization to help families fight the pressures of a worldly culture.

Every year since 1950, the United States president and all fifty governors have signed a proclamation encouraging Americans to pray for their nation on the first Thursday in May. Vonette Bright had been chairwoman of this effort, and upon her retirement, she urged Shirley to take the post. At the onset, Shirley refused, but after praying about it, she accepted the position of chairwoman of the National Day of Prayer.

Shirley has received many honorary awards and degrees. In 1996, she was designated the Church Woman of the Year. Besides leading America in the annual Day of Prayer, she authored two books with Gloria Gaither on strengthening family ties by creating and observing family traditions.

Prayer was never an afterthought in Shirley Dobson's Christian walk, and neither should it be for any believer. Fervent, sincere prayer is the very foundation for our lives. God promises to bless the person, the family, and the nation that prays.

HANNAH ADAMS

Author (1755–1831)

These also are sayings of the wise:
To show partiality in judging is not good.
PROVERBS 24:23 NIV

Hannah Adams became interested in writing when one of her father's students gave her a dictionary of all the religions from the beginning of time. She noticed the author treated most religious faiths with prejudice and even hostility.

In 1778, Hannah began to compile her own reference book of religions, based not on opinions or biases, but on factual information. This wasn't her only reason for attempting to publish a book, however—her family also needed the money.

In 1784, Hannah published *An Alphabetical Compendium of the Various Sects Which Have Appeared from the Beginning of the Christian Era*. The first edition sold out, but because of an unscrupulous agent, Hannah received little pay for her book.

While Hannah taught school to supplement the family income, she published a history of New England. She went on to author *History of the Jews, Letters on the Gospels*, and *A Dictionary of All Religions and Religious Denominations*. Hannah Adams was the first American woman to make a living as an author. In all her writings, she did extensive research and attempted to write truthfully.

It is difficult to be free of biased opinions when people's

views differ from yours. We don't do this by compromising our beliefs, but by respecting what others believe. Our only debt to others—whether or not their opinions agree with ours—is to love them.

VICTORIA

English Queen (1819–1901)

"Because of me, kings reign, and rulers make just laws. Rulers lead with my help, and nobles make righteous judgments."
PROVERBS 8:15–16 NLT

When thirteen-year-old Victoria visited industrial towns in Wales, she was horrified to see ragged, hungry children living in wretched huts black with coal dust. The trip marked the beginning of a social conscience for the young woman destined to become queen of the British Empire.

Upon the death of her uncle, King William IV, eighteen-year-old Victoria was informed she was queen. Before her coronation in Westminster Abbey in 1838, she requested two hours of solitude to pray for divine wisdom.

Two years later she fell in love with Prince Albert, her cousin. Because Victoria was the queen, she had to propose marriage to Albert. He accepted, and the royal couple enjoyed a happily married life for twenty-one years.

A well-educated man, Albert encouraged his wife to engage in worthwhile activities—and together they crusaded against slavery, child labor, and dueling. The couple eventually had nine children and, as they devoted themselves to their family, they became role models for other British families.

Although the monarchy had little power at this time, the queen was consulted on world and domestic affairs. Appalled by the living conditions of England's poor, she supported the Mines Act of 1842, which banned women and children from working underground. By 1870, education was compulsory for all British children. Students not belonging to the Church of England had been banned from attending Oxford and Cambridge Universities, but through Victoria's influence the schools were open to all.

Victoria's reign was a time of great expansion for the empire. Britain was at the height of the Industrial Revolution and became the foremost world power. Her navy ruled the seas. A missionary fervor also swept the nation during this era. David Livingstone and others left Britain's shores, taking the gospel to far-off places. Great religious groups like the Salvation Army were founded to help the poor.

One Sunday, after hearing a sermon at St. Paul's Cathedral, Victoria asked the chaplain if a person could be absolutely sure of his eternal safety. "No one can be absolutely sure," she was told. John Townsend, a Christian, heard of the queen's question and wrote her a letter in which he quoted John 3:16 and Romans 10:9–10. Soon thereafter, Mr. Townsend received a letter from Victoria. She had read the verses and wrote, "I believe in the finished work of Christ for me and trust by God's grace to meet you in that home of which He said, 'I go to prepare a place for you.' "

Seven assassination attempts were made on the queen's

life during her reign. Yet she did not appear moved by the narrow escapes. Her courageous spirit only made her more popular with her subjects.

Victoria and Albert's fourth son, Leopold, was a hemophiliac. The queen anguished over her son's condition but was comforted when, at Albert's suggestion, she spoke openly to her subjects of Leopold's malady.

In 1861, at age forty-two, Prince Albert became ill with typhoid fever. In a few days he died. Victoria could not be consoled—and for two years, she refused to appear in public. She dressed in black for the remainder of her life.

Before Victoria's reign, English people had little respect for the throne. By her decency, honesty, dignity, and sense of duty, Victoria made the monarchy respectable and created standards for future royal conduct. At her Diamond Jubilee in 1897, it was said no one in the empire was more admired than Queen Victoria. The entire time period was named after her: the Victorian Era.

Although she had worn black since the death of her husband, Victoria requested the dark color not be used at her burial. Instead, her body was dressed in white and she wore her wedding veil.

One good woman doing what was right—promoting and demonstrating a wholesome, godly lifestyle—influenced an entire nation to pursue righteousness. We, too, have a sphere of influence. As we stand on the side of good, many will be persuaded to follow in our steps.

LILLIAN TRASHER

Founder of Assiout Orphanage in Egypt (1887–1961)

He took the children in his arms,
put his hands on them and blessed them.
MARK 10:16 NIV

As a young girl growing up in Florida, Lillian Trasher wanted to marry and have children. When she became engaged to a young preacher, it seemed her dream would become a reality. Ten days before their wedding, however, Lillian attended a missionary service and received a call to missionary work.

Without a sponsoring mission board, Lillian sailed for Egypt in 1910. One day a dying mother gave Lillian her three-month-old infant. When Lillian brought the baby home, fellow missionaries told her to take the child back. She informed them the mother was dead. Lillian managed to rent a house and began gathering in homeless children. That was the beginning of Assiout Orphanage.

Although Lillian did not marry or have children, fifty years after coming to Egypt, she could look out the orphanage window and see hundreds of "her" children being fed, educated, and taught the Bible. During her lifetime, Assiout Orphanage cared for more than twenty-five thousand Egyptian children.

Children are often the object of neglect and abuse. They need to feel the strong arms of Jesus encircling them. As we pray for children, teach them God's Word, and tenderly care for them, we become His arms of blessing.

BEVERLY LAHAYE

Founder of Concerned Women for America, Author
(1929–)

*"You will receive power when the Holy Spirit comes on you;
and you will be my witnesses in Jerusalem,
and in all Judea and Samaria,
and to the ends of the earth."*
ACTS 1:8 NIV

One day in 1979, Beverly LaHaye listened to a television interview featuring a feminist who promoted anti-God and anti-family views. The speaker claimed to speak for America's women. Beverly knew the woman did not speak for *all* the nation's women, and certainly not for her. *Who will speak for America's Christian women?* Beverly asked. She decided that she would be their voice.

Beverly organized Concerned Women for America in 1979. The mission of the organization is to promote biblical principles through prayer and education. Members seek to influence society and reverse the decline of moral values in the nation. They promote sexual abstinence and support crisis pregnancy centers. The women also educate people in their communities concerning the harmful effects of drugs, pornography, and a homosexual lifestyle.

The organization has more than five hundred thousand members and includes women in all fifty states and every religious denomination. Their headquarters are in Washington, D.C., where leaders often testify before the U.S. Congress on issues such as the sanctity of human life, education, pornography, and religious freedom.

As a young woman, Beverly had attended a Christian college where she met and married Tim LaHaye, who planned to be a minister. While the couple served a church in California, Beverly heard a teacher speak about the abundant Christian life and being filled with God's Holy Spirit. She asked God to fill her, and her life changed dramatically. Once plagued with low self-esteem, Beverly believed God had equipped her to do a work through the Holy Spirit's power. Soon she would need that power as she organized women to combat the forces of evil threatening America.

Beverly believes that whatever a woman's calling is, she needs the Holy Spirit's help. She says, "The missing dimension in the feminist movement is the Holy Spirit. . . . I know how this changed my life and what the Holy Spirit will do for others." She explained her experiences in the book *The Spirit-Controlled Woman*. Beverly also coauthored a fiction series with Terri Blackstock, the Seasons Series. The books blend Christian values with real-life situations.

Child-rearing challenges, caring for older parents, stretching the budget, and being a single parent are only a few problems women face today. As Beverly LaHaye asked the third person of the Trinity to indwell and help her, so we can also ask the Holy Spirit to fill us so we can positively and powerfully influence those in our communities, schools, and churches to remain true to biblical principles.

MARJORIE SAINT VANDERPUY

Missionary (1923–2004)

*Even when I walk through the dark valley of death,
I will not be afraid, for you are close beside me.*
PSALM 23:4 NLT

On January 8, 1956, Marjorie Saint sat by the two-way radio waiting for the signal that let her know her husband and four other young missionaries were safe. The contact never came. The five men had been murdered by the Auca Indians in the Amazon jungle while attempting to bring them the gospel. In spite of the intense sorrow she felt, Marj knew God had a plan.

Marj was a student nurse when she met Nate Saint, who planned to be a missionary pilot. After she and Nate married, they moved to Ecuador—and while her husband delivered supplies to jungle locations, Marj charted his course on the radio.

After Nate's death, Marj and her three young children moved to Quito, Ecuador, where she worked as a nurse in the World Radio Missionary Fellowship hospital. In Quito she also met and married missionary Abe VanDerPuy.

From the ashes of tragedy, Marj rebuilt her life. She counseled others who had experienced losses, and reared her children so they loved those who had killed their father.

We never know when tragedy may strike our lives. Yet we need not fear the unknown future—Christ promises to walk close beside us through life's dark valleys.

HENRIETTA MEARS

Christian Educator, Author (1890–1963)

*"Go and make disciples of all the nations. . . .
Teach these new disciples to obey all the commands I have
given you."*
MATTHEW 28:19–20 NLT

When Henrietta Mears was born, the doctor told her mother the child had extremely poor eyesight and would be blind by age thirty. Yet the child went on to become one of the greatest Christian educators of the twentieth century, influencing many young people to become active in Christian ministries.

Henrietta was greatly influenced by her mother, who taught a Bible class and was reported to spend one or two hours a day in prayer. In spite of poor eyesight, Henrietta graduated from the University of Minnesota and took a job teaching high school chemistry. During this time, she also took on the task of teaching a Sunday school class of eighteen-year-old girls who called themselves "The Snobs." Under Henrietta's teaching, the class grew to more than five hundred members.

While spending time in California in 1928, Henrietta had lunch with a pastor who invited her to become the director of education at his church. As the two talked, it became evident to Henrietta that God was opening a new door of service for her.

At that time the Sunday school attendance at Hollywood Presbyterian Church was about four hundred. In two and a

half years, that number soared to more than four thousand—
and the congregation needed more rooms for classes. This
was not a problem for Henrietta, who slated classes to meet
in homes and nearby schools. Clearly, Sunday school in
America was entering a new and exciting era.

One day, as Henrietta looked over the Sunday school
material for the primary department, she noticed it had no
pictures, was not closely graded, nor was it Christ-centered.
She wrote a few lessons and mimeographed them for the
next Sunday. Soon she was writing lessons for other classes.
Churches in the area heard of her lessons and wanted copies.
Eventually she founded Gospel Light Press, which produced
Bible-based, Christ-centered, child-focused, closely graded
lessons.

As the Sunday school grew, Henrietta was faced with
the dilemma of obtaining trained teachers. She told those
she trained, "The key is in one word—work. . . . Wishful
thinking will never take the place of hard work." No matter how gifted a person claimed to be, Henrietta insisted
potential teachers have a relationship with Christ. She
further urged the teachers to completely surrender to the
Holy Spirit. Henrietta told her workers, "The building of
a Sunday school is a long road, and there are many climbs
and turns, but the rewards are worth the effort."

In the 1930s and '40s, Henrietta could be seen riding
in the back of a cattle truck taking a load of young people
to the beach or mountains as she began camping programs.
Her goals for her camps were the salvation and Christian
growth of each camper, as well as development of vision for
the world. At camp, she addressed subjects such as evolu-
tion, miracles, prophecy, and the deity of Christ. In the

early days, the camps were held at various sites, but later a resort—Forest Home Christian Conference Center—was purchased.

Perhaps Henrietta's greatest impact worldwide was through the college students she instructed. She told them, "What does God want you to do? Meet Him face-to-face and you will find out." While Henrietta served at the Hollywood church, more than four hundred young men who attended her classes answered the call to serve churches. Others went as missionaries. Bill and Vonette Bright, who founded Campus Crusade for Christ, lived with Henrietta for ten years while they began their ministry. She also counseled evangelist Billy Graham during a difficult time in his ministry.

Henrietta was not an ordained minister, nor did she have a theology degree—but she did have a heart brimming with love for God's Word and the desire to share it with every person. All believers should seriously consider their part in instructing the next generation in the truths that will transform their lives and, in the end, bring them into Christ's glorious eternity.

EVELYN LETOURNEAU

Wife and Mother (1900–1987)

*She extends a helping hand to the poor
and opens her arms to the needy.*
PROVERBS 31:20 NLT

While R.G. LeTourneau moved mountains with the giant earthmoving machines he invented, his wife, Evelyn, moved mountains of loneliness and poverty by the love that flowed from her heart and hands.

As a young couple, Evelyn and R.G. were indifferent to God and faith. But when their son died from influenza in 1918, they gave their lives to Christ and changed their priority from "things" to God.

The LeTourneaus began working in a church, and R.G. built a twenty-four-foot trailer so Evelyn could transport children to Sunday school and summer camps. During World War II, her home became a "home away from home" for servicemen.

When R.G. invited thirty homeless boys to work for him, Evelyn made room for them in her three-story home. Through the fifty-two years of their marriage, she housed and cared for many young men attending LeTourneau College, the school R.G. founded. While under her roof, she encouraged them to go to church and live for God. Because of her practical, hands-on work, Evelyn LeTourneau was chosen American National Mother of the Year in 1969.

When we ask God to use us, He often directs us to

help, feed, house, and clothe the needy. Thus we become Christ's extended hands.

ROSA PARKS

Mother of the Civil Rights Movement (1913–2005)

"For the time is coming," says the LORD,
"when I will place a righteous Branch
on King David's throne. . . .
He will do what is just and right throughout the land."
JEREMIAH 23:5 NLT

One courageous act by one courageous woman—that's all it took. But it was enough to begin a movement that created a more just life for thousands of African-Americans living in America's South.

On December 1, 1955, Rosa Parks left her job as a seamstress in Montgomery, Alabama, and boarded a city bus. She dropped into a seat in the back reserved for black people like herself. When a white man came on the bus, there was no place for him, and the driver asked black passengers to give their seat to him. Rosa didn't move and was arrested. She said at that time, "I was tired of giving in to white people." As word of Rosa's courageous stand for justice spread throughout Montgomery, black leaders decided to boycott the bus system.

December 5 was chosen as the day no black person would ride the buses. The effort was successful and led the city's black leaders to work for desegregation of the bus system, allowing them to sit wherever they desired. For over a year, no black person rode the buses. Because they comprised 66 percent of the buses' customers, the company was forced to cease operations.

During this time, Rosa received threatening phone calls. She feared for her life and her family's lives. She and her husband lost their jobs. Yet, as news of the Montgomery boycott spread around the world, Rosa received letters of support from as far away as Ghana and France. On November 13, 1956, justice prevailed when the United States Supreme Court declared bus segregation unconstitutional.

Injustice had always been part of Rosa's life. As a child growing up in Alabama, she had noticed black children walked to school while white children rode buses. Rosa's school had been a one-room building without glass in the windows, while the school for white students was a sturdy, brick structure. Yet Rosa was happy living on a small farm with her mother and grandparents. Before going into the cotton fields, her grandmother read the Bible. They attended nearby Mount Zion African Methodist Episcopal Church. Her grandfather took her fishing. He also taught her to stand up for her rights. Although she had little to do with white people during her childhood, she did not grow up hating them.

When Rosa completed sixth grade, her mother sent her to live with relatives in Montgomery where she attended Alice White's school for girls. The school, taught by white teachers, instilled in Rosa a sense of dignity and self-respect. Yet, outside the school, Rosa saw injustice in action. Black citizens drank from separate public water fountains and were not allowed to eat in restaurants marked with WHITES ONLY signs.

At nineteen, she married Raymond Parks who worked as a barber while Rosa took a job as a seamstress. She also joined the National Association for the Advancement of Colored People, an organization of black people that sought equality for their race. Rosa was appointed the organization's secretary.

After the bus incident, Rosa continued to get threatening phone calls, and she doubted if she could get work in Montgomery. In 1957, she, with her husband and mother, moved to Detroit, Michigan, where they found work.

In 1996, Rosa was awarded the Presidential Medal of Freedom by President Bill Clinton. She was also honored when Cleveland Avenue in Montgomery was renamed Rosa Parks Boulevard.

As a result of Rosa's brave act, justice for African-Americans has improved. They vote in elections without harassment and are elected to public office. There are no COLORED signs on water fountains and WHITES ONLY postings in restaurants in Southern states. And in 2008, Americans elected the first African-American to the presidency.

However, in the hearts of some people, prejudice and hatred for other races still exist. That, too, can change as they allow Christ, the just One, to live within. And someday when He appears, perfect justice, love, and equality will prevail for all peoples. *Even so, come, Lord Jesus!*

MARJORIE HOLMES

Author (1910–2002)

Elijah was as human as we are,
and yet when he prayed earnestly
that no rain would fall, none fell for
the next three and a half years!
Then he prayed for rain, and down it poured.
JAMES 5:17–18 NLT

Marjorie Holmes's purpose for writing *Two from Galilee*, a fictionalized account of the lives of Mary and Joseph, was to make the Holy Family as real to readers as the folks next door. With her thirty books and numerous magazine articles, Marjorie attempted to clear away the mystery surrounding Jesus, the Bible, and spiritual concepts, making God accessible and alive to the average person.

Marjorie was born in Iowa and graduated from Cornell College. In the 1940s, she published her first novel, *World by the Tail*. She also wrote a column, "Love and Laughter," for a Washington, D.C., newspaper, which especially appealed to homemakers.

Marjorie is best known for her trilogy, *Two from Galilee*, *Three from Galilee*, and *The Messiah*—all written in the 1980s. After the death of her husband, she wrote books about grief and healing. She also taught classes on writing and received numerous awards for her works.

With her books, Marjorie Holmes took Bible characters off their pedestals so readers could see them as real people. They overcame daily struggles using the same weapons available to us: prayer, God's Word, and faith in a caring heavenly Father.

KAY ARTHUR

Bible Study Leader and Author (1933–)

"My thoughts are completely different from yours,"
says the LORD.
"And my ways are far beyond anything you could imagine."
ISAIAH 55:8 NLT

After Kay Arthur became a Christian, her dream was to become a missionary. She achieved this goal in 1965 when she and her husband Jack and sons went as missionaries to Mexico. But after three years, Kay developed an infection in the lining of her heart, and the family was forced to return to Tennessee.

Kay grieved, prayed, and wept. "I mourned the fact I had taken a much needed man off the mission field." Jack had worked with the Pocket Testament League in Africa and South America. Now the couple was on the shelf.

Back in the United States, Jack became the manager for a Christian radio station, and Kay started a Bible study for teens in her living room. The study group grew, and the Arthurs purchased a chicken farm where the young people studied the Bible in a barn.

Then Kay began a women's Bible study. Seeing their wives' enthusiasm, husbands asked to attend. The studies grew, and it was necessary to train others to lead classes.

From this, Kay developed a method of inductive Bible study known as Precept upon Precept.

Churches and groups in the United States began using her studies. Next the lessons were sent to Korea, Mexico, and Romania. Before long, Kay's Bible study method had reached 114 countries and was published in sixty languages.

Kay's early adult life wasn't so glorious. As an attention-starved young woman, she sought love in the wrong places and ended up miserable. A friend told her she needed Jesus, and Kay finally told God, "I don't care what You do to me. . . if You'll just give me peace." Kay said she went down on her knees a harlot and came up a saint. At that moment, God set her apart for Himself.

Kay received an intense hunger for the scriptures. She would prop her Bible up on the car's steering wheel and attempt to read it as she drove to work. She said, "When the Holy Spirit comes inside you, He takes the veil off the Word of God."

Kay Arthur has published thirty-six books in forty-eight languages. More than four million copies of her Bible study courses are in print. A radio broadcast, *Precept with Kay Arthur*, is heard on as many as two hundred stations. She also has a weekly call-in program, *Precept Line with Kay and Jan*.

Kay thought she knew God's purpose for her life, but He had a better idea. As we keep our hearts open to the bigger picture—God's will—His plans may also be a delightful surprise to us.

⋆ HELEN BARRETT MONTGOMERY ⋆

Author, Church Leader (1861–1934)

> *"He is Lord over all lords. . .and his people
> are the called and chosen and faithful ones."*
> **REVELATION 17:14 NLT**

Which is more important: faithfulness to God's work or success in the work? Helen Montgomery achieved both. She has been described as "a woman of ten talents who used them all."

In 1924, Helen translated the Greek New Testament into English, the only woman to publish such a work. She was also licensed by her church to preach—and, at age forty-nine, she became the president of the Northern Baptist Convention, another first for a woman.

An ardent supporter of missions, Helen raised large sums of money for mission causes and traveled the world to observe the work of missionaries. For one project, Seven Colleges for Women in Asia, Helen solicited funds from American women and built Christian colleges in Japan, China, and India.

Perhaps the greatest demonstration of Helen's faithfulness was seen in her service to her church in Rochester, New York, where for forty-four years, she taught a women's Bible class that numbered more than two hundred attendees each Sunday.

No doubt Helen Montgomery heard Christ's "well done" when she entered heaven. As we strive to faithfully do God's work, we will also hear those words when we bow before His glorious presence.

GLADYS AYLWARD

Missionary (1902–70)

In your strength I can crush an army;
with my God I can scale any wall.
PSALM 18:29 NLT

Gladys Aylward stood on the platform of the Liverpool
Street Station in London, an old fur rug draped over her
arm. Beside her was a suitcase filled with crackers, tins of
corned beef, baked beans, and fish. Her clothes, bedding,
and cooking utensils were wrapped in a blanket.

It was October 18, 1930—and the tiny, twenty-eight-
year-old woman was leaving England for China. Rather
than take a ship, she chose the cheaper route overland by
rail through Europe and Russia.

Two years earlier when Gladys had applied to a mission society for an appointment to China, she was told,
"Your qualifications are too slight, your education limited.
The Chinese language would be far too difficult for you to
learn."

While those words sounded in her ears, another voice
said, "Gladys, millions of Chinese have never heard of Jesus
Christ."

Convinced that God had called her, Gladys worked as
a maid and saved her money for the fare. After traveling
by train, boat, and mule, Gladys arrived at the home of
Jeannie Lawson, a seventy-four-year-old missionary living in
Yangcheng, a city in northern China.

"How shall we live with no money?" Gladys asked the

older missionary one day. While Mrs. Lawson received a small amount of support, Gladys had no income. Mrs. Lawson, who had recently purchased an old house, suggested they turn it into an inn. The mule trains would stop there, and after the men were fed, she would tell them Bible stories.

At first Gladys fed the mules while Jeannie Lawson told the stories. In a year's time, Gladys began telling the muleteers about Jesus—and one of the men became her first convert.

A year after Gladys's arrival, Mrs. Lawson died. Gladys managed to keep the inn going, but without the second income, there wasn't enough money to buy food.

One morning, Gladys heard a commotion at the gate of the inn, and the mandarin—the highest ranking official in the district—entered the courtyard. He had received a letter from the Central Government demanding the custom of binding women's feet to cease. He asked Gladys to find a woman to do the inspections.

In a month's time, Gladys had not found a foot inspector, and when the mandarin returned, he told her to take the job. "If I inspect feet, I will also tell the people about God," she said. Because the mandarin believed a man's gods were his own affair, Gladys was hired. Her salary was one measure of millet a day and a farthing.

With soldiers to protect her from robbers, Gladys went from village to village. During the day, she inspected feet—and in the evening, people gathered as she told them about Jesus. With the salary she received, she was able to stay in Yangcheng and keep the inn operating.

One morning, Gladys was summoned to the men's

prison. A riot had broken out, and the governor of the prison asked Gladys to stop the fighting. When she voiced her fears to the governor, he reminded her that she had told everyone, "The living God protects me."

What Gladys saw in the prison courtyard horrified her. Bodies of the dead and wounded lay on the flagstones. A convict, flashing a bloodstained chopper, stopped a few feet from Gladys. When she demanded the weapon, he took two steps closer and meekly held out the ax. Not only was the riot stopped, but Gladys was able to bring reform to the badly managed prison. Soon the prisoners were weaving and tending gardens.

When Japanese planes dropped bombs on Yangcheng in 1938, Gladys guided nearly one hundred children on a twenty-eight-day march over the mountains before the advancing Japanese army. Later she went to Taiwan to work with refugees and orphans.

The woman who was told she could not learn the Chinese language mastered six Chinese dialects. You may have others around you saying you are unqualified for the job God has asked you to do. However, whether you are called to be a more effective parent, begin a new ministry, or share Christ with a neighbor, God is your source. With His help, you can scale any wall.

DOROTHEA DIX

Humanitarian, Teacher, Nurse (1802–87)

*Dear children, let us not love with words
or tongue but with actions and in truth.*
1 JOHN 3:18 NIV

In 1841, Dorothea Dix volunteered to teach a women's Sunday school class at the East Cambridge, Massachusetts, House of Correction. What she saw disturbed her. The women—many mentally ill—were confined in unheated smelly cages, closets, cellars, stalls, and pens. They were chained, naked, beaten with rods, and lashed into obedience. Dorothea brought the abuses to the attention of the state's court—and, in time, they were corrected.

In the next four years she visited jails and almshouses in every state east of the Mississippi River and took detailed notes. Everywhere Dorothea traveled, it was the same: Prisoners, the mentally ill, and disabled people were treated harshly. She pled before state legislatures, and as a result, she helped establish thirty-two mental hospitals and fifteen schools for the mentally disabled. When she was commended for her efforts, she said, "I am merely acting in obedience to the voice of God."

Dorothea Dix believed every person has value, and she worked to see that those unable to speak for themselves received fair treatment. Certain groups of people in our communities may also be neglected. We can do something. We may call their need to the attention of those who can help. And we can show God's love to them by becoming actively involved in their lives.

MAHALIA JACKSON

Gospel Singer (1911–72)

Commit everything you do to the LORD.
Trust him, and he will help you.
PSALM 37:5 NLT

She was called "Queen of Gospel Music," recording thirty albums during her career—including a dozen that sold over a million copies. Some regard her as the greatest gospel singer in history. Yet Mahalia Jackson did not have a great beginning.

Besides her mother and preacher father, several aunts and cousins lived with the Jacksons in a three-room house in a poor neighborhood of New Orleans. Mahalia sang in a children's choir in her church—and even then, she was greatly influenced by the popular jazz music of the city. When her mother died, five-year-old Mahalia and her brother went to live with their Aunt Duke, who did not allow secular music to be played in her home. There Mahalia made a commitment to sing only gospel music.

At age sixteen, Mahalia moved to Chicago where she worked as a laundress for a dollar a day. She became involved in a church choir and was soon singing in storefront churches and tent revivals. In 1948, Mahalia recorded "Move On Up a Little Higher." The record sold a million copies, and Mahalia rocketed to fame. She toured the United States and Europe, singing in concert halls. Her rendition of "Silent Night" became one of the bestselling singles in the history of Norway.

Mahalia had her critics, however. More formal congregations disapproved of her exuberant singing, a combination of gospel and jazz. The remarks didn't change her clapping, swaying, shouting performances. She said, "I want my hands, my feet, my whole body to praise God." Jazz recording companies tried to lure her with lucrative contracts, and family members urged her to try other types of music, but she refused. Neither would she sing the popular blues music of the time. She said, "Gospel songs are songs of hope. When you sing them, you are delivered from your burden."

Mahalia became the first gospel singer to perform in Carnegie Hall. In 1961, she sang at President John F. Kennedy's inauguration. Before Dr. Martin Luther King gave his "I Have a Dream" speech, Mahalia sang a Negro spiritual. At his funeral five years later, she sang her signature song, "Precious Lord, Take My Hand."

Early in her career, Mahalia Jackson made a commitment to sing only gospel music. She never compromised this vow to her "precious Lord," and God honored her with success. The Lord takes our commitments to Him seriously. When we make and keep promises that honor God, He will also crown our efforts with success.

MARY BUNYAN

Wife, Mother (1625–56?)

You are the light of the world—like a city on a mountain, glowing in the night for all to see.
MATTHEW 5:14 NLT

Mary could not read or write. A poor woman, she did not have a dowry when she married John Bunyan, the rowdy, blaspheming tinker (maker and mender of utensils). But she was a godly woman, and she brought two books to their marriage: *The Practice of Piety* and *The Plain Man's Pathway to Heaven*. As John read them to her, he became interested in his wife's faith.

Mary attended church and continued to live by biblical principles in her home, which eventually led to her husband's conversion. However, Mary's life did not become easier with John's change of heart. Now he began to preach—and because this was illegal for those not ordained by the Church of England, John was often in jail. There he wrote *Pilgrim's Progress*, a book destined to become a classic Christian work.

Mary managed the household and cared for the couple's four children, including a blind child, while John spent most of twelve years in prison.

Mary Bunyan's life is an example of faith in action. How can we more effectively influence others for God? The same way Mary did. Our godly lives will serve as a light, pointing them to Jesus, the Light of the world.

SUSANNA WESLEY

Teacher, Author, Mother (1669–1742)

*Teach your children to choose the right path,
and when they are older, they will remain upon it.*
PROVERBS 22:6 NLT

Susanna Wesley was beset by many problems while raising
her family. Nine of her nineteen children died soon after
birth. One infant was accidently smothered by a servant.
Her oldest son didn't talk as a child. After Susanna "prayed
day and night," at age five he said his first words. When
troubles increased, this mother spent more time in prayer.

Described as a beautiful young lady, Susanna Annesley
was the twenty-fifth child born into a pastor's family in
England. Susanna's home was filled with good books; and
she learned to read Hebrew, Greek, and Latin. She could
also discuss theology with any preacher.

At thirteen, Susanna met Samuel Wesley, who became a
minister in the Church of England. They married when she
was nineteen.

The couple's first pastorate was a rural church in South
Ormsby, where the manse was a one-room mud hut with a
loft. Lack of money was always a problem for the Wesleys.
Once, when Samuel was put in prison because he could
not pay his debts, Susanna sent him her wedding ring so
he'd have something to barter for food. After eight years
in South Ormsby, Samuel accepted a church in Epsworth,
where an increase in salary helped meet the needs of the
growing family.

Susanna was the primary source of her children's education and taught them Latin, Greek, French, Logic, the Bible, and Christian conduct. Classes were held six hours daily, six days a week. She wrote three textbooks: commentaries on the Apostles' Creed, the Lord's Prayer, and the Ten Commandments. Susanna said the purpose of her children's education was the saving of their souls.

A devoted mother, Susanna spent time alone with each child during the week. Monday was given to John, Tuesday to Hetty, and so on until each child had one-on-one time with his or her mother. The large household also had strict rules of discipline. The children were taught to cry softly and to eat whatever was set before them. No child got his or her way by whining.

Susanna gave two hours each day to private devotions. With the children's education, household duties, and tending to the cows, pigs, and hens, how did she find time for personal meditation? She would throw a large apron over her head, and in the midst of the noisy household, she prayed.

Trouble was never far from Susanna. On two occasions, the Wesleys' home burned to the ground. During one fire, a six-year-old son narrowly escaped death when he was rescued through an upstairs window. After the incident, Susanna gave special attention to this child so divinely protected. John Wesley went on to become the founder of the Methodist Church.

Susanna and Samuel had strong opinions—and when they disagreed about a particular political matter, Samuel left his wife and family for one year, vowing never to return until Susanna changed her views.

During her husband's absence, Susanna began a Sunday afternoon religious service in her home for the family. The small congregation sang a psalm, prayed, and listened while Susanna read a sermon. Soon neighbors asked to join the group. Eventually, more than two hundred people gathered while Susanna shared the gospel with them. When England's political situation changed, Samuel returned home.

After her husband's death, Susanna lived with various children. She stood in fields and listened to her sons John and Charles preach to thousands of England's poor. She sang the songs Charles wrote to instruct converts in worship. As she lay dying, she told her children, "As soon as I am released, sing a psalm of praise to God."

Initially, Susanna's godly influence was confined to her family. Soon her faith impacted her neighbors. However, because of her well-taught children, the whole world eventually felt God's love through Susanna Wesley, a preacher of righteousness.

Most mothers can't hope to accomplish all Susanna did. Yet, as we teach our children by word and example, the Bible promises they will remain on the right path and, by their righteous lives, positively influence others.

LETTIE COWMAN

Author, Missionary, Evangelist (1870–1960)

*"There's a young boy here with five barley loaves and two fish.
But what good is that with this huge crowd?"*
JOHN 6:9 NLT

When Charles Cowman became seriously ill, his wife, Lettie, gathered short inspirational writings to read to him. From that small beginning, her collection of poems and prose became the book *Streams in the Desert.* Lettie's book has been published in more than one hundred English printings and is translated into fifteen languages. Chinese leader Chiang Kai-shek requested her book be buried with him.

Lettie and Charles Cowman went as missionaries to Japan in 1900 and founded the Oriental Missionary Society. Their goal was to place a scripture portion in every home in the empire. When Charles died, Lettie became president of the society. She befriended national leaders, preached around the world, and wrote Christian books. Today the mission society she and her husband founded is one of the major missions.

Small things! A boy gave his lunch to Jesus. We share a few dollars with a missionary or a homeless person. We discount little kindnesses, thinking they don't matter. Though Lettie Cowman had no thought of sharing her writings with the world, God had other plans, and her books have blessed generations. Our kind deeds, too, have that potential.

FLANNERY O'CONNOR

Author (1925–64)

Where sin abounded, grace did much more abound. . . .
even so might grace reign through righteousness
unto eternal life by Jesus Christ our Lord.
ROMANS 5:20–21 KJV

The *New York Times* said of Flannery O'Connor, "Her talent for fiction is so great as to be overwhelming." Flannery received a passion for writing while attending Georgia State College for Women where she was part of the yearbook staff and editor of a literary magazine. After graduation, she attended the famous writers' school at the University of Iowa, where she began her first novel, *Wise Blood,* which was published in 1952.

Often violent, Flannery's novels showed flawed, ignorant, religious characters transformed by pain and conflict. As a Catholic living in the Protestant South, her stories deal with racial issues, poverty, religion, and the Holocaust. She said, "My subject in fiction is the action of grace in territory held largely by the devil." Using foreshadowing and suspense in her stories, Flannery's books keep the reader turning pages.

A student of the Bible, Flannery wrote slowly and prayerfully, listening to the inner voice. She believed that her talent was God-given and that she was responsible to develop and use it to honor God. She painstakingly edited and rewrote her works until a perfect story with believable characters emerged. Through fiction, she showed readers the struggles of life and ultimate triumph of those who trust God.

In many ways, Flannery's stories are a reflection of her life. She was devastated when her father died from lupus when she was fifteen. At age twenty-six, she was diagnosed with the same disease. Upon receiving the news, she moved back to her ancestral farm in Georgia, where she wrote and also raised various kinds of fowl. Fascinated by birds, Flannery incorporated them into her stories. Though often weak during the course of the disease, she was able to write two to three hours a day and completed two novels and thirty-two short stories. Flannery also wrote numerous letters that give insight into her deep Christian beliefs. At the onset of lupus, she was told she had five years to live— yet she lived several years beyond that prediction.

Flannery died at age thirty-nine. While her writings received little recognition during her lifetime, she is now considered one of the most important American writers of the twentieth century.

Flannery wrote in a letter, "Grace changes us and change is painful." Through trouble and conflict we often feel the "grace of God" working in our lives. We can thank God for these difficulties. They are evidence of His powerful efforts to transform us to be like Christ and, at life's end, take us to be forever in His presence.

JOSEPHINE BUTLER

Crusader for Women (1828–1906)

"For I, the LORD, love justice.
I hate robbery and wrongdoing."
ISAIAH 61:8 NLT

Injustice in any form made Josephine Butler's blood boil!
Even as a child, she wanted everyone treated fairly. After
the tragic death of her six-year-old daughter, Josephine
began a campaign against an injustice prevalent in the
world: prostitution.

Josephine longed to "rescue fallen women for
Jesus," but her friends were shocked when she took the
unfortunate women into her home. Later she founded
House of Rest, a home for girls in danger of falling into
prostitution.

Her greatest fight was against the Contagious Disease
Act, an effort to legalize prostitution in cities occupied
by military troops. While people of the time often called
prostitutes "the sewers of society," Josephine knew women
entered this lifestyle because of poverty, force, or lack of
education.

Josephine's crusade spread to Europe, and she helped
establish the first international movement to aid prostitutes.
She dared speak against an evil and addressed large audiences at a time when prostitution was considered a shame-
ful topic to discuss and women were expected to remain
silent on public issues.

Because many people find it convenient to ignore evil,

it will never be easy to confront injustice. Yet the down-trodden often lack a voice. Perhaps you and I can speak for them in our communities.

SOJOURNER TRUTH

Evangelist, Abolitionist (1797?–1883)

"Love one another. As I have loved you,
so you must love one another.
By this all men will know that you are my disciples,
if you love one another."
JOHN 13:34–35 NIV

Mau Mau Bett, a slave mother, couldn't give her thirteen children much—but she loved Jesus and passed His love on to them.

Often her child Isabella would slip away to an alcove of willows to pray. She would soon need the strength of those prayers when, at about age nine, she was sold for one hundred dollars and a flock of sheep. In the new place, Isabella was whipped regularly—and for the remainder of her life bore the scars.

When the treatment became unbearable, she prayed for deliverance. Her owner eventually died, and she was sold to a tavern owner. When this man fell on hard times, Isabella was again sold. Her treatment at the hands of John Dumont and his wife was harsh and, besides daily humiliations, may have included sexual abuse.

As a young woman, Isabella fell in love with Robert,

a slave on a neighboring farm. Dumont forbade the relationship, and after Robert visited Isabella one night, his owner beat him savagely in the face and sent him away. From this relationship, Isabella had a daughter. In 1817, she was forced to marry an older slave named Thomas, and the couple had four children. Isabella became heartbroken when her owner illegally sold Peter, her five-year-old son.

John Dumont had promised to free Isabella—but when the time came, he refused. Bitter, filled with raging hatred, Isabella decided to escape with her infant. As she fled, she prayed and eventually stumbled onto the home of Isaac and Marie Van Wagenen. When Dumont demanded the return of his slave, the Van Wagenens paid him twenty dollars for her services for a year. The couple insisted Isabella call them by their first names rather than master and mistress—and, for the first time, she received kind treatment from white people.

While living with the Van Wagenens, Isabella attended the Methodist Episcopal Church and experienced a life-changing conversion. During this time, she also appealed to the Quakers, who helped her seek the return of Peter. After months of legal proceedings, a scarred and battered son returned to his mother. In 1827, New York emancipated all slaves, and Isabella, now free, took a job as a servant.

In 1843, she received a call from God to preach the gospel. Isabella changed her name to Sojourner Truth and began traveling throughout New England on foot, preaching in camp meetings and churches. A tall woman with a deep voice, her preaching included stories from her slave days—and in spite of the harsh treatment she'd received most of her life, she spoke of "God's mystical love." As she preached, she would often break into song, singing of her freedom in Jesus.

During her travels, Sojourner met prominent abolitionist Frederick Douglass, who asked her to appear with him in abolition rallies. Although Sojourner couldn't read or write, she began dictating her memoirs. In 1850, her story, *The Narrative of Sojourner Truth*, was published. The book provided her with an income and opened the door for Sojourner to preach, recount stories of her slave days, and sell her books.

During the Civil War, Sojourner gathered supplies for black soldiers. One day, while working with refugees in Washington, D.C., she visited President Lincoln and had her picture taken with him. He showed her a Bible he had received from the black people in Baltimore, and she had him sign her autograph book. He wrote, "For Aunty Sojourner Truth. October 29, 1864. A. Lincoln." After the war, Sojourner helped ex-slaves find jobs, and she worked for temperance causes and women's rights.

Most of her life, Sojourner received cruel treatment, which resulted in a fiercely bitter woman. That changed when she was touched by God. From then on, His love flowed through her, even to those who had treated her harshly. If we find it difficult to forgive people for past wrongs, we, like Sojourner Truth, can go to Calvary. Jesus has plenty of love to share with us—at His cross.

SARAH ADAMS

Hymn Writer (1805–48)

Come near to God and he will come near to you.
JAMES 4:8 NIV

Was it a spiritual experience that prompted Sarah Adams to write the powerful hymn "Nearer, My God, to Thee," or did a scripture one day suddenly jump off the page and speak to her? No one knows for sure—but looking into her life, we find clues for her inspiration.

Young Sarah believed God's truth could effectively be conveyed on the stage, and she aspired to be an actress. Ill health prevented her from reaching this goal, and she turned to writing to express her faith. Yet sickness and discouragements were never far away. The English poet Robert Browning was greatly used to encourage her, and it is believed she received the inspiration for her famous hymn through his influence.

The hymn has blessed many, including England's Queen Victoria and King Edward VII. When United States President William McKinley lay dying from an assassin's bullet, he quoted Sarah's hymn and told the doctor, "This has been my constant prayer."

You *can* draw near to God. Say the name of Jesus. Whisper a prayer or quote a verse of Sarah Adams's hymn:

Nearer, my God, to Thee,
Nearer to Thee,
E'en though it be a cross

That raiseth me!
Still all my song shall be:
Nearer, my God, to Thee;
Nearer, my God, to Thee,
Nearer to Thee.

BETTY STAM

Missionary Martyr (1906–34)

You will keep in perfect peace all who trust in you,
whose thoughts are fixed on you!
ISAIAH 26:3 NLT

When missionary John Stam inquired whether it was safe
to take his wife and child into Tsingteh, a Chinese village,
he was assured Communist activity was not a threat. Yet,
while Betty and John passed out tracts and held meetings in
the small city, rumors of nearby rebel activity persisted. On
December 6, 1934, a frightening message reached them:
Enemy soldiers were approaching. When the Stams realized
it was too late to flee, they calmly knelt in prayer and committed their lives to God.

Betty Scott met John Stam at Moody Bible Institute.
Her parents were missionaries to China, and Betty also felt
called to missions. She and John fell in love—but because
the call was their priority, marriage was not in the near
future. Betty went to China, and John followed in a year.
They met in Shanghai and were married. A year later, their
child, Helen Priscilla, was born.

That day in December, communist soldiers burst into the Stams' home, bound John, and took him away. Later they came for Betty and the baby. While John and Betty's fate was sealed, the soldiers questioned what they should do with the baby. When a soldier suggested killing her, a bystander offered to die in her place. Soon the man was dead.

While held hostage in an abandoned mansion during the night, Betty managed to feed her daughter and wrap her securely. The next morning, the couple was ordered to leave the baby. They were stripped of outer clothing and marched through the village to the taunts of onlookers. At a spot outside town, while a crowd looked on, an acquaintance of the Stams pled for their lives. The man admitted he was a Christian and was swiftly killed. When the sword struck John, Betty fell over his body. Then it was her turn.

Upon hearing of John and Betty's deaths, Mr. Lo, an evangelist, was told the location of their child. Although she'd gone two days without food, little Helen Priscilla was well. Mr. Lo quickly transported the baby to missionaries a hundred miles from Tsingteh. Then he faced the grim task of burying the bodies of Betty and John Stam.

How did Betty Stam maintain peace of mind when she, her husband, and their child were almost certain to perish? No doubt, she fixed her mind on God. Could we be as courageous under the same circumstances? God's strength does not come before it is needed. At the exact moment, we, too, will have strength to face severe adversity should that be our fate.

ELIZABETH FRY

Prison Reformer (1780–1845)

*"Whatever you did for one of the least of these brothers of mine,
you did for me."*
MATTHEW 25:40 NIV

When Elizabeth Gurney was eighteen years old, a Quaker friend told her, "You are born to be a light to the blind, speech to the dumb, and feet to the lame." This prediction saw fulfillment one day in 1817 when Elizabeth visited the women in London's Newgate prison. Three hundred women and their children were crowded into four small rooms. They slept on straw. The smells were unbearable, the language foul. The women and children existed on a pitifully small amount of food.

That day Elizabeth, in her plain Quaker dress, opened her Bible and read to the women. On her next visit, she was accompanied by her Quaker friends who brought clothes and supplies to teach the women to sew.

At that time, selected women criminals were transported to a penal colony in Australia. Elizabeth and her friends visited the ships before they sailed and gave the women cloth and thread so they could make items to sell once they reached their destination.

Other countries heard of Elizabeth's reform efforts and sought her advice to assess their prison systems.

Christ commands His followers to help the outcasts. Unbelievable as it seems, when we visit, clothe, and feed them, we actually do the kind deeds to Jesus.

MADAME JEANNE-MARIE GUYON

French Mystic, Author, Hymn Writer (1648–1717)

*You should be known for the beauty that comes from within,
the unfading beauty of a gentle and quiet spirit,
which is so precious to God.*

1 PETER 3:4 NLT

At age ten, Jeanne-Marie Bouvier de la Motte's aristocratic,
well-to-do French family placed her in a convent, where
she spent time studying the Bible and memorizing scripture
verses. During this time, she also vowed to do the will of
God in everything. She wanted to become a nun. But when
Jeanne was sixteen, her mother arranged for Jeanne's marriage to a wealthy, older, handicapped man, and she became
Madame Guyon. Because of a cruel, domineering mother-
in-law, it was not a happy situation—yet Jeanne learned
to submit to keep the peace. In the early years of marriage,
she contracted smallpox, which left her face permanently
scarred.

After twelve years of marriage, Madame Guyon, at age
twenty-eight, was left a widow with three small children.
Concerned for her spiritual welfare, she counseled with a
Franciscan priest who advised her to "do what our Lord
has made you know He desired of you." Her heart was
changed, she turned her back on Paris's social life, refused
offers of marriage, and spent her time studying devotional
books and caring for her children.

At age thirty-four, she began what she called "an apos-
tolic life." In the next eight years, Madame Guyon traveled

through villages in France and Switzerland teaching rich and poor alike how to pray and encouraging them to live holy lives. Often, her life was in danger as she traveled, and on one occasion, her carriage was stopped by robbers. When the men opened the carriage door, they fled when they saw a woman in black smiling at them.

Madame Guyon found a great spiritual hunger for her teaching of Quietism, which renounced creeds and works, emphasizing passive contemplation, meekness, and contentment in all circumstances. She gave out food, took the sick and dying into her home, and eventually founded two hospitals.

Madame Guyon's activities soon caught the attention of the church. The authorities—jealous of her popularity—said she was out of order to pray and preach. Didn't she know only priests were to pray, not women?

During this time, monasteries were off-limits for women—yet Madame Guyon gained entrance and proclaimed her faith to the monks. She also preached in nunneries. A nun, contemplating suicide because she felt she couldn't be reconciled to God, consulted with Madame Guyon, who assured her she could rely on Christ's righteousness. Healing miracles often accompanied Madame Guyon's ministry, and she claimed to have visions. While she remained faithful to the Catholic Church, officials continued condemning her actions and placed her in a prison cell in the Bastille—an imprisonment that continued for seven years. The last two years were spent in solitary confinement. Yet she didn't complain and spent her time singing, praying, and writing. She believed Christians should pray at all times, and she wrote *The Method of Prayer*, based on 1 Thessalonians 5:17, "Pray without ceasing" (KJV). Most of her writing was done at night, and she claimed God wrote the books through her. From a cell, she eventually wrote forty books. The church condemned these books and publicly burned some copies.

While in prison, Madame Guyon also wrote hundreds of hymns. Her best-known hymn, "O Lord, How Full of Sweet Content," written in 1681, was translated into English by William Cowper. She said of her time in prison, "There is nothing for me to do but adore Thee and carry my cross." Because she had learned to quiet her inner self, she calmly bore her imprisonment.

Later John Wesley studied Madame Guyon's twenty-volume commentary on the Bible and said she was an example of true holiness. Adoniram Judson, missionary to Burma, also read her books and imitated her meek acceptance during his two years in prison.

Though her face was scarred by smallpox and lined from multiple trials, Jeanne Guyon exuded an inner beauty. As we spend time in Christ's presence, as we absorb the truths of His Word and pray for a calm spirit, we, too, will show forth the glory of a Christlike countenance and life.

IDA SCUDDER

Medical Missionary (1870–1960)

The Holy Spirit said,
"Dedicate Barnabas and Saul
for the special work I have for them."
ACTS 13:2 NLT

Young Ida Scudder had no intention of becoming a missionary to India as three generations of Scudders had done. She'd rather do "something exciting." But while helping her mother in India, a Brahmin man came to Ida asking help for his fourteen-year-old wife, who was having a difficult labor. Ida explained she had no training, but her father, a doctor, would help. The man shook his head. His religion prohibited a man from attending a woman. That evening, two more men came to the mission with the same request. Each time, Ida sadly refused. In the morning the tom-toms tolled the deaths of the three women. As Ida searched her soul, she realized God wanted her to put aside her plans and follow His will.

Ida went to America and enrolled in medical school. She returned to India in 1900 and founded a hospital and sponsored roadside clinics, branch hospitals, training courses for girls, and a medical school.

What is God's highest design for our lives? As we pray and see world needs, we, too, will "hear" His voice telling us to put aside our petty plans for His better plan—one that will benefit many and give us a more purposeful life.

RUTH STAFFORD PEALE

Author, Wife (1906–2008)

*The LORD God said, "It is not good for the man to be alone.
I will make a companion who will help him."*
GENESIS 2:18 NLT

When Ruth Stafford was a senior at Syracuse University,
friends told her about a young minister whom they said was
"the most eligible bachelor." Ruth met Norman Vincent
Peale at a party, and when they were introduced, it seemed
he held her hand longer than necessary. After college, Ruth
took a job teaching mathematics in high school and began
dating the minister. Two years later, they married.

The Great Depression was heavy upon the nation, and
the pews were mostly empty when the young couple moved
to New York City to pastor the Marble Collegiate Church.
In an effort to increase their congregation, Ruth suggested
that Norman become more visible in the community.
When he accepted speaking engagements at area clubs and
organizations, the church gradually filled.

While Norman was a great preacher, he was not a good
organizer, nor did he enjoy business meetings. Early in
their marriage, Ruth determined to be interested in what
concerned her husband. She attended committee meetings
and reported back to Norman, freeing him to write, counsel, and prepare sermons.

Once, when Norman voiced discouragement because
of problems in the church, Ruth startled him by telling
him he needed to become converted. He assured her he

was converted. Yet his wife's remark led Norman to rethink his level of trust in God. After earnest prayer, he plunged into his work convinced that, with God's help, nothing was impossible.

When Norman submitted his book *The Power of Positive Thinking* to publishers, it was rejected numerous times. Finally, in disgust, he threw it aside. Ruth retrieved the manuscript and submitted it again. The book appeared in print in 1952 and sold twenty million copies.

Then trouble began. Prominent ministers said Norman's book did not express Christian values. When the scathing remarks became known to Norman, he was deeply hurt. Ruth advised her husband to counter with Christ's love. With her encouragement, Norman "outloved" his critics. Ruth shared her experiences in her books *The Secrets of Staying in Love* and *The Adventure of Being a Wife*.

In 1944, a group of people gathered around Ruth's kitchen table and planned a new magazine. The publication would relate true stories of how faith helped people in everyday life. With Ruth as executive vice president, *Guideposts* hit the newsstands in 1948. The magazine eventually became the most widely read religious inspirational magazine in the world.

When a wife actively supports her husband, she is also realizing her God-appointed destiny—to be a helper to the man she loves.

MARY LYON

Christian Educator (1797–1849)

Fear of the LORD is the beginning of wisdom.
Knowledge of the Holy One results in understanding.
PROVERBS 9:10 NLT

In 1834, Mary Lyon began an arduous journey: She would go to New England villagers and farmers and solicit funds to begin a women's college. *Whoever heard of women attending college?* many asked. Most people of the time thought women needed only basic reading, writing, and arithmetic skills, if even that.

In spite of poor health, for three years Mary persisted—and Mount Holyoke Female Seminary opened its doors in 1837. Mary's initial order of business for the eighty young women in the first class was to challenge them to become Christians. Besides a rigorous curriculum in languages, science, and literature, the students were instructed in the benefits of a balanced diet and exercise. Mary's educational purposes were clear: The women were to be educated so they could evangelize the world.

Her efforts were effective. By the time of her death, seventy graduates had gone to foreign mission fields, and many more were missionaries to the American Indians.

Mary Lyon recognized that true knowledge begins with recognizing God and knowing Christ as our Savior. From that point on, all knowledge we acquire is filtered through God's powerful book of wisdom—the Bible.

MARY SMITH MOFFAT

Missionary (1795–1870)

*What is faith? It is the confident assurance that what we hope
for is going to happen.
It is the evidence of things we cannot yet see.*
HEBREWS 11:1 NLT

As apprehensive parents waved good-bye, an excited young
woman, Mary Smith, boarded a ship in London bound for
South Africa. *Will we ever see our daughter alive again?* the
Smiths wondered. Probably not. Most white people didn't
live long on the Dark Continent. Their daughter did not
entertain such dismal thoughts. Mary only knew that after
a three-month voyage to Cape Town, she would be with her
beloved Robert.

The couple had met in Scotland when Robert Moffat
worked as a gardener for Mary's father. Both were dedicated
Christians. Both felt called to mission work. When he proposed marriage, Mary's parents said no. In 1816, Robert
sailed for Africa alone. Later Mary's parents changed their
minds—and in 1819, she followed Robert.

The romance of missions quickly faded as Mary and
Robert set out by oxcart on a six-hundred-mile journey
inland. After crossing raging rivers and evading giant ant-
hills, Mary found herself living on the edge of a parched
desert in Kuruman with a totally degraded people. When
she went to church, she carried her pots and pans with
her lest the natives steal them. The garden Robert so
proudly cultivated was also subject to thievery. Yet she

wrote, "When I sit in the house of God surrounded by the natives. . .I feel that an honor has been conferred upon me which the kings of the earth could never have done for me."

In Kuruman, Mary washed clothes in a river and made soap from sheep fat. She ground wheat for the bread she baked in an outdoor oven. As she worked to transform their one-room mud hut into a home, she cleaned her floor with cow dung to kill the fleas. Mary gave birth to ten children and raised them in the most primitive conditions. She also taught native children about Jesus.

Perhaps the most painful problem the Moffats faced in the early days of the mission was the lack of converts. After working for ten years without one conversion, the mission society considered abandoning the work. Again Mary's faith was evident as she wrote a friend: "Send us a communion service; we shall want it someday." When Robert, busy with translation work, became discouraged, she reminded him, "We walk by faith, not by sight." Always confident, she said, "We may not live to see it, but the awakening will come as sure as the sun will rise tomorrow."

The awakening came in 1828. Heathen songs and dances stopped. Long before the meetings began on Sunday, the church crowded with singing Christians. Prayers were heard, and the conduct of the natives improved.

As the church grew, so did Mary's family. Besides raising ten children of her own, Mary took in three native children who, according to custom, would have been buried alive with their dead mother.

Yet death and tragedy were never far from Mary. After

twenty years without a furlough, the Moffats embarked for Scotland. On board ship, her six-year-old died and was buried at sea. During the Moffats' time on the British Isles, Mary rarely saw her husband as he traveled promoting mission causes. She gave birth to another child while on furlough.

While Robert was in London, a young man, David Livingstone, heard him preach and felt called to Africa. Livingstone later married the Moffats' oldest daughter, Mary. At age forty, Mary Livingstone died. One of the Moffats' sons, Robert, also died young, as did a missionary daughter, Elizabeth. Four of the surviving Moffat children became missionaries.

After fifty years in South Africa, the Moffats, weak and sickly, retired to England where Mary died four years later.

Mary Moffat believed in the sun when the sky was the blackest. She learned to smile while her heart brimmed with sorrow. She lived contently in the most uncomfortable situations. By her faith, she overcame the obstacles. Mary's brand of faith is available to anyone willing to endure the rigors that allow this quality of faith to grow.

HELENA OF CONSTANTINOPLE

Mother of the First Christian Emperor (250?–330?)

I have been reminded of your sincere faith,
which first lived in your grandmother Lois
and in your mother Eunice and,
I am persuaded, now lives in you also.
2 TIMOTHY 1:5 NIV

The first three centuries were a time of intense persecution for Christians as they faced the terrors of the pagan Roman Empire. But all that changed in 312 when Emperor Constantine became a Christian. Credit for his conversion goes largely to Helena, his mother.

As a young woman, Helena converted to Christianity. She married Constantius Chlorus, who later divorced her for political reasons. After Helena's son became emperor, he restored her to court where she attempted to persuade him of the truths of Christianity.

Although not a Christian, when Constantine prayed before a critical battle, he saw a cross in the sky. Above it were the words, "By this thou shalt conquer." When the battle ended in victory for Constantine, he became a Christian and declared religious freedom for the followers of Christ.

Helena influenced her son for Christ and helped change history. We, too, have a sphere of influence. As we live our lives by Christian principles and speak of the change Jesus has brought to us, we will also affect people for Christ and His cross.

CASSIE BERNALL

Student (1981–99)

Everyone born of God overcomes the world.
This is the victory that has overcome the world, even our faith.
1 JOHN 5:4 NIV

After her death, musicians wrote songs about her; yet on the day seventeen-year-old Cassie Bernall died, she was only thinking about studying Macbeth for an English class. When two gunmen walked into the library, she said, "Dear God, what is happening? I just want to go home." A gunman slammed his hand on the table and yelled, "Peek-a-boo!" Although reports vary, witnesses say the gunmen asked several students if they believed in God. Cassie was one of the students killed in the massacre.

A casual reader of the Columbine High School massacre may not realize that Cassie was headed on the same road as her killers—but for a series of choices she had made earlier.

In her teens, Cassie turned from being a happy child into a sulking stranger. Her parents thought this was normal teenage behavior until one day her mother found letters Cassie had written to friends. The letters spoke of killing her parents and drinking blood. Sketches of vampire teeth and axes decorated the pages.

When Cassie's mother confronted her daughter, Cassie went into a screaming rage and vowed to kill herself. The parents, Misty and Bert, broke off their daughter's friendships with occult-practicing friends. The only activity they allowed Cassie outside school was attending a church youth group.

Every effort the parents made to control Cassie met with resistance. When she erupted in fits of anger, her mother or father would sit with their hand on her knee, praying aloud, telling her they loved her.

The Bernalls enrolled their two children in a private school. To escape Cassie's friends, the family moved to a new neighborhood.

One weekend, the Bernalls allowed Cassie to attend a church youth retreat. The theme for the retreat was overcoming temptations. As Cassie watched young people lay drug paraphernalia and occult materials at an altar, the walls surrounding her began to fall. When she arrived home, she told her mother, "I've totally changed."

Dressed in baggy jeans and wearing ball-and-chain necklaces, an insecure Cassie became part of a youth group. In her junior year, she transferred to Columbine High School. Friends remember seeing her reading her Bible in class. Instead of talking about vampires and death rock, she became interested in photography.

On April 21, Cassie said good-bye to her mother and went to school. She didn't return home. Two years earlier, Cassie had made the choice to overcome evil. That choice ended with her victorious home-going.

When we choose to place our faith in Christ, we, too, are promised an overcoming life—and death.

ELIZABETH HOOTEN

First Woman Preacher (1598–1672)

*Don't be surprised at the fiery trials you are going through. . . .
Instead, be very glad—because these trials
will make you partners with Christ.*
1 PETER 4:12–13 NLT

George Fox, founder of the Quakers, believed women should share equally in ministry with men. His first convert, fifty-year-old Elizabeth Hooten, felt called to preach and traveled across England boldly urging people to repent.

When Elizabeth's cattle were stolen, she appealed to King Charles II. Believing all people were equal, she refused to bow to the king—a serious crime. Rather, she used the opportunity to preach repentance to him. The king promised Elizabeth she could settle anywhere in the American colonies, but when Elizabeth arrived in New England, authorities scorned the king's letter. She received whippings in three Massachusetts towns. At one location they led her into the wilderness in the middle of winter and left her there. Elizabeth found her way back to civilization and sailed for England.

Beatings, time in prison, and abandonment in dense forest did not discourage Elizabeth. Her courage remained unshakable, and her message of repentance was given with zeal.

We can stay in our comfort zones and not voice our convictions. Yet there are times when we, like Elizabeth Hooten, need to honestly tell people the truth about God

and their eternal destiny. Be prepared: Your actions may
bring you persecution.

CATHERINE MARSHALL

Author (1914–83)

Surely your goodness and unfailing love
will pursue me all the days of my life,
and I will live in the house of the LORD forever.
PSALM 23:6 NLT

Through life's varied experiences, Catherine Marshall learned
that God makes the difference in every situation. With Him,
the word *impossible* flees. Defeat turns to victory, and what
looks like a dark future becomes bright—with God.

Catherine Wood was raised in a pastor's home in the
South during the Depression. There was never enough
money for the needs of the family of five—but because
there was plenty of love, Catherine did not know her family was poor. As a teen, Catherine had three passions: She
dreamed of becoming an author; she wanted to attend
Agnes Scott College in Decatur, Georgia; and she aspired
to marry a "wonderful man." But how could she go to college when her family couldn't even afford a car? Mother
and daughter knelt and asked God's help. A few months
later, Catherine's mother received a letter from the federal
government asking her to write a history of the county.
Catherine felt God's goodness and mercy as her mother's
project covered college expenses.

At Agnes Scott College, Catherine developed her love for writing. During her freshman year, she heard about Peter Marshall, the handsome bachelor preacher with the delightful Scottish accent. On Sundays, she often took the long streetcar ride to the Westminster Presbyterian Church in Atlanta to hear him. Catherine was smitten by the silver-tongued preacher, but so were other girls. Rationalizing her attraction was only a schoolgirl's crush, she tried to stay away from the church but was always drawn back.

Was it her imagination that the young pastor's eyes seemed to seek her out during his sermon? Soon he asked to drive her back to college—and in her senior year, he proposed. With marriage and the arrival of a son, Peter John, Catherine realized more of God's goodness and mercy.

When Peter John was three, Catherine was diagnosed with tuberculosis and ordered to stay in bed. She asked God to heal her, but her health did not improve. As she studied her Bible one night, Christ's presence filled her bedroom and He assured her, "There is nothing wrong with you that I can't take care of." After three years, her health improved.

But a greater challenge followed when her husband, Peter, died of a heart attack at age forty-six. As Catherine pondered how a thirty-four-year-old widow with a nine-year-old son could make a living, a verse from Psalm 23 came to mind. *Goodness and mercy from Peter's death?* she wondered. When a publishing house asked her to compile a book of Peter's sermons, *Mr. Jones, Meet the Master* soon appeared in bookstores. Then Catherine wrote *A Man Called Peter*, the story of her husband's life. The book remained on the *New York Times* bestseller list for more than fifty consecutive weeks.

As a young woman, Catherine's mother had taught school in the Great Smoky Mountains of eastern Tennessee. Her experiences became the basis for Catherine's book *Christy*, which sold more than eight million copies. Other books followed.

In spite of success and the busyness of raising her son, Catherine was lonely. Suitors pursued the eligible young widow, but it was Len LeSourd, a *Guideposts* editor with three young children, who captured her heart.

As Catherine tackled the job of blending two families into one, rejection by Len's children was just one problem she faced. Seeking solutions, Catherine and Len agreed to attack their difficulties using God's weapon of prayer. All their prayers weren't answered as they desired, yet answers eventually came. Again, Catherine experienced goodness and mercy.

When two grandchildren—Peter John's children—died shortly after birth, Catherine asked, "Is God in everything?" When she looked for answers in the long shadows of life, she found comfort.

With her faith firmly in God, Catherine Marshall trusted Him in life's good times and the difficult places. In every instance, she experienced goodness and mercy. We, too, will sense the Lord beside us at every bend in the road if we keep our faith anchored firmly in Christ.

DOROTHY SAYERS

Novelist, Playwright (1893–1957)

"Love the Lord with all your heart and with all your soul and with all your strength and with all your mind."
LUKE 10:27 NIV

Dorothy Sayers felt a responsibility to use her talents to influence as many people for Christ as she could. Witty and outspoken, she did this in a variety of ways.

Her father, a minister, surrounded his daughter with good books—and, in a loving home, Dorothy became a Christian. Later she declared it made more sense to be a believer in Christ than a heretic.

After graduating from Oxford University, Dorothy became friends with C. S. Lewis, J. R. R. Tolkien, and other Christian writers. When she wrote and published sixteen detective novels, she achieved celebrity status in England. She did a series of radio plays of the life of Christ entitled *The Man Born to Be King*. Her book *The Mind of the Maker* is considered her best work and expresses biblical truth in a unique way. Dorothy also made a translation of Dante's *Divine Comedy*.

Working passionately, Dorothy used her talents to their full potential to allow the light of Christ to shine in a dark world. Our passion determines what we do and how we do it. As we are passionate for Christ, we'll use our gifts, laboring for His cause and for others who do not know Him.

LAURA INGALLS WILDER

Author (1867–1957)

For the word of God is full of living power.
It is sharper than the sharpest knife,
cutting deep into our innermost thoughts and desires.
It exposes us for what we really are.
HEBREWS 4:12 NLT

The winter of 1880–81 was severe for the community of De Smet in Dakota Territory. The little town experienced a blizzard almost every day until snow reached the roofs of the houses, and food and fuel supplies ran dangerously low. As the winds raged, thirteen-year-old Laura Ingalls read her Bible and memorized scripture verses. This was not a new activity for Laura. When the family lived in Minnesota, she had memorized one hundred verses to win a competition in a Methodist church. These verses became the sustaining force for Laura as she faced other "storms" of life.

The Ingalls family had experienced troubles of all kinds during Laura's growing-up years. In Minnesota, a plague of grasshoppers came through and devoured their crops. It was repeated the next year. To supplement the family income, Laura, at age twelve, took a job caring for an ill neighbor. Away from home, she became homesick. As she prayed, she felt a "hovering Presence, a Power comforting and sustaining."

Laura's sister Mary became blind as a result of scarlet fever. To help pay Mary's tuition to an Iowa school for the blind, Laura, at fifteen, took a job teaching school.

Even after Laura married Almanzo Wilder, the couple's life was a round of disappointments. Their second child died soon after birth. The house Almanzo had built burned to the ground. Hard times struck again when Laura and her husband became ill with diphtheria, from which Almanzo never regained his strength.

When the family moved to the milder climate of Missouri for Almanzo's health, money was scarce. Laura raised chickens and wrote a column for the local newspaper to make ends meet.

Laura never intended to become a noted author. She *was* concerned that the way of life she had known on the American frontier would be forgotten, and in an effort to preserve it, she began writing stories of her youth. When Laura was sixty-five years old, her first book, *Little House in the Big Woods*, was published.

Where did Laura receive strength to overcome the years of adversity? How do we survive the cruel twists of fate that often come our way? The Bible verses Laura had learned as a child gave her courage and strength during the hard times. *God's Word is full of living power!* As we read its promises and trust in God, we, too, will come through on the other side of adversity into overcoming victory.

MARY ANN PATON

Missionary (1840–59)

"Blessed are the dead who die in the Lord. . . .
they will rest from their labor,
for their deeds will follow them."
REVELATION 14:13 NIV

Some people are highly influential during their lifetimes.
Others wield the greatest influence after their death. This is
the case with Mary Ann Paton, who died at age nineteen.

Fourteen days after their wedding in 1858, Mary
Ann and John Paton sailed from Scotland for missionary
work in the South Pacific. What they found on the island
of Tanna shocked them. The "painted savages," most of
them nude, were untouched by civilization. Fierce tribes
struggled for control of the island. After killing their
victims, they cooked their bodies and ate them. In this
harsh land, Mary Ann gathered eight women to instruct
in Christian teaching. Three months after arriving, Mary
Ann gave birth to a son. She then contracted a tropical
fever and soon died.

After Mary Ann's death, missionaries on the island
passed a resolution that read: "Her earnest Christian
character, her devoted missionary spirit, her excellent
education. . .excited expectation of great future usefulness."

Mary Ann Paton's brief life echoes down through the eons
of time, reminding us that it is not so important how long we
live, but that in the time we are given, by faithfulness, goodness, and love, our lives produce fruit that lasts forever.

ELISABETH ELLIOT

Missionary, Author (1926–)

*"You will receive power when the Holy Spirit comes on you;
and you will be my witnesses in Jerusalem, and in all Judea
and Samaria, and to the ends of the earth."*
ACTS 1:8 NIV

In January 1956, Elisabeth Elliot's husband, with four other missionaries, was speared to death in the Amazon jungle. The killers, from a tribe deep in the rain forest of Ecuador, were the Auca Indians, who avoided contact with white men and other Indian tribes.

Elisabeth Howard had grown up in a mission-minded family. She read missionary biographies and attended services in which missionaries showed slides of their work. From these mission workers, Elisabeth learned of the hardships of their work. She also had a good ear for languages—and when she heard there were more than two thousand language groups in the world without the Bible in their tongue, she thought she might help decrease that number.

While at Wheaton College, Elisabeth felt a definite call to Bible translation work. Jim Elliot, a fellow student, also felt called to the mission field.

After graduation, Elisabeth attended the Summer Institute of Linguistics under Wycliffe Bible Translators. She continued to correspond with Jim after they both went to work in different areas as translators to Ecuador's Quichua Indians. In January 1953, they married. Their daughter, Valarie, was born in 1955.

While working with the Quichuas, Jim—with Nate Saint, Pete Fleming, Roger Youderian, and Edward McCully—attempted to make contact with the Auca Indians. Flying over the jungle settlements, the men dropped gifts from the plane as a show of friendliness. On January 8, they landed their Piper by the Curarey River and met two Auca men and a woman. The missionaries were promptly speared to death.

Shock waves rippled around the world when the deaths were reported. Elisabeth and the other wives clung to each other for comfort. For Elisabeth, this was not a tragedy. She said, "God has a plan and purpose in all things." Jim had loved the Aucas, and Elisabeth's love for them intensified after her husband's death. There was no doubt in her mind what she would do: She was called to be a witness.

Shortly after the spearing, Elisabeth, her three-year-old daughter, Valarie, and Rachel Saint, the sister of Nate Saint who also was killed, made plans to go to the Aucas—now known as Huaorani. They lived with them and attempted to reduce their language to writing in order to translate the Bible into their language.

If a language is to be reduced to writing, the translator must first find an informant—someone who knows the language and is willing to help. As Elisabeth prayed for such a person, two Auca women appeared at the mission station. They invited Elisabeth and Rachel Saint to live with them.

Moving deep into the Amazon jungle, the women went to a remote Auca village with no modern conveniences. They lived in a hut with only a roof to protect them from torrential tropical rains and, for the most part, ate what the villagers ate. They swam and fished with the Aucas. Elisabeth struggled to reach across the communication barrier, while Valarie quickly learned the language.

Elisabeth lived with the Aucas for two years, perfecting her language skills. Wycliffe Bible Translators then became involved, and nine years after the slaying of the five missionaries, the Gospel of Mark was printed in the Auca language.

Elisabeth and Valarie returned to the Quichua work and remained there until 1963, when they came to the United States. In the ensuing years, Elisabeth wrote more than twenty books. She also served as a stylist consultant for the New International Version of the Bible committee, and today she is in demand as a speaker.

Power to go, power to tell. For more than fifty years Elisabeth received power to go and tell. She told the most primitive Indian tribes of the Amazon jungle. With her superb writing skills, she told the world's enlightened population. The command to "go" is to all believers, even you and me. Changing lives is also our goal.

MONICA

Mother of Augustine (331–87)

*Pray at all times and on every occasion
in the power of the Holy Spirit.
Stay alert and be persistent in your prayers
for all Christians everywhere.*
EPHESIANS 6:18 NLT

Is prayer an effective way to change a wayward heart?
Monica, a Christian mother, prayed year after year for her
prodigal son—and her prayers were eventually answered
when God touched Augustine's heart and, through him,
the entire world.

Before her son was born, Monica consecrated him to
God's work. She warned young Augustine of the evils of
the age, but he paid no attention. At sixteen, he was a thief
and deceiver. In his teens, he took a mistress and had a
child with her. Augustine later wrote he "walked the streets
of Babylon in moral filth." Monica consulted with a bishop
who advised her to "only pray God for him."

One day, Augustine heard a voice repeatedly say, "Take
it, read it!" He took this to mean the book of Romans.
When he read Paul's admonition to make no provision for
the flesh, Augustine believed. A changed man, he became
a leader in the church, and his writings profoundly influenced later Protestant reformers.

Persistent, continued prayer is a tool every believer can use
to change the heart of one person, a family, a community—
the entire world. *Pray on!*

GLORIA GAITHER

Musician, Songwriter, Author (1942–)

Worship the LORD with gladness;
come before him with joyful songs.
PSALM 100:2 NIV

Gloria Gaither has written lyrics for more than six hundred songs, many of which have become gospel classics. With the Gaither Trio, she has recorded more than sixty albums. She is the lyricist of twenty songs that received the Gospel Music Association's Dove Award, and the author of twelve books and a dozen musicals. Six universities have awarded her honorary doctorate degrees. Yet Gloria and her husband, Bill, claim to be "just plain folks."

As a preacher's daughter growing up in Michigan, Gloria Sickal wanted to be involved in Christian ministry. She attended Anderson College in Indiana and majored in French and sociology with plans to go to Africa as a missionary.

When Gloria was a junior in college, she met Bill Gaither, an English teacher. As they dated, he talked about the gospel songs he'd written, and she showed him her poetry. After their marriage, they became soul mates, working together to compose songs. Soon their music opened doors for concerts and recordings. Much credit for the popularity of gospel music today goes to Gloria and Bill as a result of their Homecoming concerts and videos.

Where does Gloria get the ideas for her songs? Many come from life experiences. In the 1960s, with two young children, Gloria became pregnant with a third child. The "God is dead" theory was rampant at that time, and she wondered if it was wise to bring children into such a world. Noting their doubts and problems, a friend prayed with Gloria and Bill, and hope revived. After the birth of a healthy child, the lyrics to "Because He Lives" flowed from Gloria's grateful heart.

A student of literature and a lover of words, ideas for songs come to Gloria from a phrase of a sermon, a line in a prayer, or a thought in a scripture verse. Her book *We Have This Moment* is based on years of personal journaling.

In the 1980s, the Gaithers began a television show— *The Gaither Gospel Hour*—which includes a touring schedule. Sometime later came *Homecoming*, a magazine that includes information of concerts, videos, and stories about the musicians.

In spite of success in gospel music, Gloria believes relationships with family, friends, and her Lord are more important than fame. She freely gives her time, love, and attention to their three children, six grandchildren, and Jesus, her Savior, through prayer and Bible reading.

The psalms encourage us to sing joyful songs. Gloria Gaither's lyrics help us to do just that, and future generations will be inspired to sing joyfully because she poured out her soul in heartfelt, inspiring verses.

EVANGELINE BOOTH

First Female General of the Salvation Army
(1865–1950)

Whatever your hand finds to do, do it with all your might.
ECCLESIASTES 9:10 NIV

From childhood, Evangeline Booth's parents taught her to serve God and others fervently. As a young woman, she worked in the slums of London. A many-talented person, she played the harp and wrote hymns. At age thirty-one, she became commander of the Salvation Army in Canada and Newfoundland. She led the United States Salvation Army for thirty years, and in 1934 she became the Army's first female general. Her father, William Booth, rightfully described his daughter when he said, "The best men in the Army are the women."

During World War I, the public's respect for the Army soared when Evangeline sent officers to France to support the troops. Her "Doughnut Girls" brought the Salvation Army worldwide fame as female officers fried and served doughnuts to soldiers close to the front. Returning veterans praised their efforts. When disasters, earthquakes, famines, and fires occurred, Evangeline quickly sent food and relief. Because of her humanitarian efforts, President Woodrow Wilson bestowed upon her the Distinguished Service Medal.

Evangeline burned brightly for others, making a difference in the world. Like her, we can develop and use our talents for the good of humankind. The world will be a better place when we do.

Author, Hymn Writer (1811–96)

Righteousness exalts a nation,
but sin is a disgrace to any people.
PROVERBS 14:34 NIV

In 1793, the American Congress passed the Fugitive Slave
Act, which said fugitive slaves had to be returned to their
owners. As slavery issues became heated in the mid-1800s,
the Fugitive Slave Law of 1850 was passed, and anyone
feeding or sheltering a slave was fined a thousand dollars.
All over the North, law officers looked for and were paid
bonuses for finding runaways—sometimes based only on
unsubstantiated claims of ownership. As a result, even free
black people living in the North were sometimes captured
by slave hunters and shipped south in chains.

The law infuriated many Northern people, especially
those who wanted slavery abolished. The most unlikely
person to do anything about the unfair law was a woman.
Yet that is exactly whom God chose to call attention to the
sordid injustices of slavery.

In 1850, Harriet received a letter from her sister-in-law
Isabella, who told Harriet she should write something to
call attention to the law. That day, the mother of six vowed,
"I will write something. I will—if I live." Yet for months
Harriet's mind was blank. One day while sitting in church,
a vision formed in her mind. She saw an old slave named
Tom asking God to forgive his tormentors as he was being
whipped. Harriet accepted the vision as from God. She

hurried home and scribbled words on scraps of paper. She later said the Lord wrote the book and she merely transcribed His words. *Uncle Tom's Cabin*, a novel uncovering the horrors of slavery, first appeared as a magazine serial. In 1852, it was published as a novel—and, in one week, the book sold ten thousand copies. It was later translated into seventeen languages.

Harriet Beecher was one of nine children born into a distinguished clergyman's family in Connecticut. When she was four, her mother died and Catherine, an older sister, took over the household. At an early age, Harriet memorized more than twenty-five hymns and long passages from the Bible. When she was twelve, she committed her life to Christ during a church service.

As a young woman, Harriet taught in a seminary for females operated by Catherine. When her father became president of a theological seminary, Harriet and her family moved to Cincinnati, Ohio. Across the river in Kentucky, slavery was legal—and, for the first time, Harriet saw the effects of the slave system. There she married Calvin Stowe, a professor in the school and an outspoken opponent of slavery.

As the seminary enrollment decreased, Calvin was paid little and the family was besieged by poverty. To supplement their pitiful income, Harriet took in boarders and, at one time, started a small school. Harriet also wrote and sold her work to help support her family, which, by 1847, included five children with another child on the way. Later she wrote dramatic serials for a magazine.

Uncle Tom's Cabin gained Harriet fame and provided opportunities for her and Calvin to speak at antislavery rallies. Harriet prayed her book would also heal the differences of America's North and South. Instead, it helped fan the strife between the two sections and culminated in the Civil War. When President Abraham Lincoln met Harriet in 1862, he said, "So this is the little lady who made this big war."

The Civil War touched Harriet deeply when her son, Fred, was wounded. He also suffered from alcoholism and later moved west. His family never heard from him again.

God is concerned that all people are treated justly. Harriet Beecher Stowe's book, America's first protest novel, called attention to the horrible injustice of one man owning another and helped abolish slavery from America's soil. Other unjust practices continue in our world. These, too, need to be highlighted. We can do this in a variety of ways: by voting for fair laws, speaking out against society's evil practices, and even with our pens. Like Harriet Beecher Stowe, we can do our part to see that all men and women are treated with dignity and fairness.

CATHERINE OF SIENA

Reformer (1347–80)

*"Love the Lord your God with all your heart
and with all your soul and with all your mind."*
MATTHEW 22:37 NIV

Catherine was the twenty-fifth child born into a Christian family in Italy. As her family gathered every evening for prayer, she developed an intense love for Jesus. At age six, she received a vision of Christ.

When she told her parents she must spend time alone with God, they made a small room for her where she fasted and prayed. During her teen years, her parents encouraged her to marry, but she vowed to dedicate her life to God. She spent three years in seclusion, and at age sixteen, she was ready to begin her mission to serve people.

Catherine visited prisons and comforted criminals at their executions. When the Black Death swept through Siena killing hundreds, she nursed the sick.

This was a time of unparalleled corruption in the church, and Catherine dared to confront queens, kings, and popes with the truth of God. Her message: There are two realms—one of darkness, the other of light. She urged leaders to choose light. Yet Catherine's call to purity was for the most part ignored.

As we read the Bible, one command stands out: *Love God with our entire being.* Catherine heeded this admonition. We also do well to make love for God our aim.

HELEN STEINER RICE

Poet (1900–81)

"Don't be afraid of what you are about to suffer. . . .
Remain faithful even when facing death,
and I will give you the crown of life."
REVELATION 2:10 NLT

Helen Steiner Rice believed much of life consists in carrying crosses, and she had many to bear. She also asserted a Christian's cross eventually leads to a crown.

When Helen Steiner was sixteen, her father, whom she adored, died in the 1918 flu epidemic. With this loss, Helen's plans to attend college were dashed. To help support her family, she took a job making lampshades. This led to work as an advertising manager for a company where Helen met Franklin Rice, a wealthy banker. In 1929, they married; and the couple enjoyed lavish homes, luxury cars, and servants. This ended with the stock market crash later that year when Franklin lost his money—and in 1932, he took his life. After Helen paid the family's debts, she had little left.

Helen took a job writing greeting cards for Gibson Art Company. She soon became the editor of the company and stayed at this post for forty-two years. During this time she wrote thousands of poems. Her books of poetry eventually sold nearly seven million copies.

When Helen wrote a line of Christmas cards that expressed deep spiritual insights, her fame as a greeting card writer soared. And when she combined her poem "The

Praying Hands" with Albrecht Dürer's drawing *Praying Hands*, it became the most popular greeting card ever issued.

In 1960, Helen's poem "The Priceless Gift of Christmas" was read on a national television show, and her dream to share the true message of Christ's birth was realized when thousands of listeners wrote asking for a copy of the poem.

Helen's first book, *Just for You*, published in 1967, launched her to international fame. Other books followed. All her books express Helen's deep devotion for Christ. She said, "I believe in miracles. I believe in prayer. I know God is the answer to everything."

As Helen's greeting cards and books became popular, letters came to her from all parts of the world, and the writers often shared their problems. Helen advised one depressed person to read the Twenty-third Psalm very slowly with deep meditation. Helen said, "You can heal your body and mind and heart with this psalm."

Crosses too heavy to bear. Most people experience heartbreaking crosses during their lifetimes. A verse from Helen's poem "Let Not Your Heart Be Troubled" gives "cross bearers" good advice.

> *Whenever I am troubled*
> *And lost in deep despair,*
> *I bundle all my troubles up*
> *And go to God in prayer.*

With prayer and faith in God, our crosses lead to crowns.

CHRISTINA GEORGINA ROSSETTI

Poet, Hymn Writer (1830–94)

There is only one God and one Mediator
who can reconcile God and people.
He is the man Christ Jesus.
1 TIMOTHY 2:5 NLT

Christina Rossetti wrote more than nine hundred poems in English and six hundred in Italian, as well as three books of poetry, four books of devotions, and six hymns. She has been called one of the greatest English female poets of all time. Also a devout Christian, Christina poured her deep faith into her writings.

Christina was raised by godly parents. Her mother read to the children from the Bible and *Pilgrim's Progress*. Her father, a poet and university professor, died suddenly—and the family was stricken with sorrow and, eventually, poverty. At age fourteen, Christina's faith was further tested when she suffered a nervous breakdown.

She was engaged to marry on two occasions, but Christina didn't go through with either wedding for what she called "religious reasons." Instead, she focused on writing devotional material and children's poetry. Christina's devotion to Christ is reflected in her poem "None Other Lamb":

None other Lamb, none other name,
None other hope in heaven or earth or sea,
None other hiding-place from guilt and shame,
None beside Thee.

Christina's poem assures us that there is only one bridge across life's inevitable heartaches. There is only one way to God's peace—through Jesus, the Lamb of God.

AMY CARMICHAEL

Missionary, Author (1867–1951)

Jesus said, "Let the children come to me. Don't stop them!
For the Kingdom of Heaven belongs to such as these."
And he put his hands on their heads and blessed them.
MATTHEW 19:14–15 NLT

As Amy Carmichael grew up in Ireland, she enjoyed a loving relationship with her Christian mother. From her, Amy also learned effective mothering skills, which she would use when she became a "mother" to India's children.

One cold day as young Amy and her brother walked home from church, they noticed an outcast woman shuffling along the road carrying a heavy burden. The two siblings rushed to aid the woman. As the wind blew the woman's rags, the three passed a stone fountain and a voice spoke to Amy. "Gold, silver, precious stones, wood, hay, stubble. . .fire shall try every man's work of what sort it is."

Amy turned to see who had spoken. No one was there; but the incident spoke to her: She was to turn from worthless things—wood, hay, and stubble—and minister God's love to outcasts.

As a young woman, Amy taught Bible studies for "shawlies"—women working in factories who wore shawls because they couldn't afford hats. Energetic and well organized, Amy's studies eventually attracted hundreds of women.

It was a time of intense missionary fervor in Great Britain. News of missionary David Livingstone's exploits in Africa were recounted in churches. Amy became acquainted with notable Christians, including missionary Hudson Taylor. When she asked God what she should do, she again heard a voice. This time it said, "Go ye."

A mission society accepted Amy, and she sailed for Japan. After a year, she became ill and transferred to Ceylon where the climate better suited her. Within a year, Amy, sick with a serious fever, returned to Ireland.

In 1895, she went as a missionary to South India. Immediately she contracted dengue fever. Amy wrote home asking for prayer as she struggled to learn the Tamil language. When her health improved and she could converse in Tamil, she, with others, traveled for seven years to small villages evangelizing women. Her motto: "Love through me, Love of God."

Hinduism, the religion of much of India, practiced temple slavery of children. Poor parents sold their boys and girls to priests for prostitution. When a slave girl named Preena fled the temple, her hands branded as punishment from previous escapes, she came to Amy. Three months after Preena's arrival, four more children appeared at Amy's door. Gradually, she realized her mission was to rescue India's children and provide a Christian home for them. Using the skills she had learned from her mother, Amy began Dohnavur Fellowship. She said of the Fellowship, "We are not an institution. We are a family."

Not everyone was happy with her rescue efforts. Her supporters said she wasn't a real missionary, only a babysitter. Others said Amy could not hope to change a centuries-old tradition such as temple prostitution. Indian authorities accused her of kidnapping, and her life was threatened. Yet to save the children became a "fire in her bones."

As Dohnavur grew, there was not enough money to provide for the children, but Amy refused to beg for funds. She simply presented the needs to God. Workers, too, were scarce—and in 1904, Amy's mother came to help her daughter.

When cholera struck a nearby village, Amy and others helped nurse the village people; yet the plague did not touch the children at Dohnavur. Other times, epidemics raged through the cottages and Amy kissed the children as they died in her arms.

A mission society asked Amy to write a book about her experiences in India. But when she wrote *Things as They Are*, the society rejected the manuscript, saying it was too dismal. Amy's friends learned of the book and had it published. In all, she authored forty books.

At age sixty-four, Amy experienced a fall and remained disabled the rest of her life. During her fifty-five years in India, she never took a furlough.

While child prostitution is now illegal in India, the world's children continue to be targeted by evil people. In some way, reach out to a child. Pray for children. *Place your hands on them.*

EUGENIA PRICE

Author (1916–96)

"My sheep recognize my voice;
I know them, and they follow me."
JOHN 10:27 NLT

Eugenia Price didn't become a Christian to escape hell or to assure herself a place in heaven. She said, "I was captivated by the One who holds 'captivity captive.' " After her conversion, she confessed, "I am His and He is mine! That is my theology. It is very simple and I have discovered. . .that it works."

Eugenia was born into a privileged family in West Virginia. In college, she studied journalism and soon was writing scripts for radio. She moved to Chicago and, from a childhood friend, Eugenia heard about being born again. Captivated by cigarettes, drugs, and drink, she resisted the salvation message. In 1949, she gave heed to Christ's voice, became a believer, and began writing scripts for *Unshackled*, a Christian radio program.

Later God led Eugenia to move to Georgia, where she wrote Christian historical novels of the area. She eventually wrote fourteen novels and twenty-six nonfiction titles. Her books repeatedly made the *New York Times* bestseller lists and sold more than fifty million copies in eighteen languages. It happened as she listened to the voice of her Shepherd.

Jesus compares His relationship to the believer as that of a shepherd to his sheep. The Shepherd calls to His sheep. Our challenge is to listen, obey, and follow our Lord.

MARY KAY ASH

Christian Businesswoman, Author (1918–2001)

"Well done, my good and faithful servant.
You have been faithful in handling this small amount,
so now I will give you many more responsibilities.
Let's celebrate together!"

MATTHEW 25:21 NLT

She has been called one of the greatest woman entrepreneurs in American history, but Mary Kay didn't set out to be the "greatest." She wanted to help women like herself succeed in the business world, and she accomplished her goal by employing the Golden Rule—"Do unto others as you would have them do unto you." She said, "I can say unequivocally that every decision we make at Mary Kay is based on the Golden Rule."

While growing up in Texas during the Great Depression, her mother often told her, "Mary Kay, you can do it!" This "can-do" attitude stuck. In spite of a failed marriage and having three children to support, Mary Kay made plans to become a doctor. Taking an aptitude test, she learned she had a gift for sales. In 1963, after a successful career in direct sales, Mary Kay decided to write a book to help other women in business. She compiled a list of positive points she had observed in companies and another list featuring ways to improve these businesses. When she read the list, Mary Kay realized she had created her own marketing plan. With her savings of five thousand dollars and the help of her son Richard, she created Mary Kay Cosmetics.

Her philosophy for the new company was God first, family second, and career third.

After achieving success, Mary Kay was often asked to autograph dollar bills. Beside her name, she'd write *Matthew 25:14–30*, the parable of the talents. She said, "I really believe that we are meant to use and increase whatever God has given us. The scripture tells us that when we do, we shall be given more."

Mary Kay received the Horatio Alger Distinguished American Citizen Award in 1978—and in 1985, she was named one of "America's 25 Most Influential Women" in *The World Almanac and Book of Facts*. In 1996, Mary Kay Cosmetics was highlighted in the book *Forbes Greatest Business Stories of All Times*.

As great as Mary Kay's achievements were, perhaps her greatest achievement was encouraging women to believe in themselves and use their talents to improve their lives. A dynamic Christian, she praised her employees and inspired them with these words: "Expect great things and great things will happen. . . . Expect a miracle every day."

God has given every person talents, and He challenges us to invest them wisely. When we use what we have, as Mary Kay did, God can then bless us with much more.

ANNA BARTLETT WARNER

Hymn Writer, Author (1827–1915)

*"If anyone gives even a cup of cold water to one
of these little ones because he is my disciple. . .
he will certainly not lose his reward."*
MATTHEW 10:42 NIV

A boy gave his lunch to Jesus, and that simple act fed
five thousand people (see John 6:9). Anna Warner took a
simple, well-known Bible truth and wrote the poem "Jesus
Loves Me." The verses, when combined with music, have
touched children and adults in every country of the world
for 150 years and remain the most popular hymn of all
time.

Anna and her sister lived near West Point Military
Academy; and for more than fifty years, they conducted a
Sunday Bible class for cadets. Both sisters became successful
novelists. However, Anna preferred writing hymns. In 1858,
she wrote her famous song.

When China was closed under communism, the world
heard little from Chinese Christians. In 1972, a letter came
through with this line, "The 'this I know' people are well."
The message passed through censors, but Christians understood the meaning.

Most of us pass through life doing simple things. We
teach a child, feed a hungry person, or care for an ill family member. These deeds done as unto Christ are promised
a rich reward. And God may use our kindness, as He did
Anna Warner's song, to feed a multitude.

CATHERINE BOOTH

Cofounder of the Salvation Army, Author, Evangelist
(1829–90)

*In all these things we are more than conquerors
through him who loved us.*
ROMANS 8:37 NIV

In Victorian England women rarely raised their voices in public and almost never preached in churches, but Catherine Booth changed that custom. Her fame as an evangelist endured for thirty years and forever altered women's roles in ministry.

Because she was a sickly child, most of Catherine Mumford's early education was done at home. Her mother, fearing worldly influences, considered the Bible and *Pilgrim's Progress* the only acceptable reading for her daughter. By the time Catherine was twelve, she had read the Bible through several times.

She said her "heart always yearned after God." However, at sixteen, Catherine experienced "a great controversy of soul" and subsequently received assurance of her salvation after reading Charles Wesley's hymn "My God, I Am Thine."

Because her father was an alcoholic, Catherine took a firm stand against alcohol. At a temperance meeting, she met young evangelist William Booth—and he made the mistake of saying he didn't believe in total abstinence from alcohol. Catherine politely attacked that idea. Later, through her influence, the Salvation Army took a firm stand against alcohol consumption.

The Booths married in 1855. In the early years of their marriage, Catherine occasionally filled the pulpit. But on Pentecost Sunday in 1860, she rose from her seat in London's crowded Bethesda Chapel and joined her husband on the platform, telling him she wanted to say a word. A surprised William Booth turned the pulpit over to his wife, and Catherine confessed that, while she proclaimed a woman's right to preach, she had never been willing to preach the gospel. Now she was willing to be "a fool for Christ."

Five years after the birth of their fourth child, she began preaching revival meetings. With the establishment of the Salvation Army, women shared equally with men as preachers and leaders.

Catherine's appearance in the pulpit was described by an observer: "Nothing could be neater, a plain black straw bonnet. . .a black loose jacket. . .and a black silk dress." Her preaching style was said to be a "calm and precise delivery."

As Catherine's family grew, so did her popularity as an evangelist. She soon filled large halls and made converts wherever she preached. A month after recovering from the birth of her sixth child, she was preaching again. In some places, there were not halls large enough to hold the crowds, and dozens of people stood outside.

Clergymen of the day regularly attacked "female ranting" in the pulpit. In reply, Catherine wrote *Female Ministry: Woman's Right to Preach the Gospel*, a pamphlet denying the charge that female ministry was forbidden in the Bible.

When Catherine and William established the Salvation

Army in 1878, she designed the army flag, inscribed with the words BLOOD AND FIRE. She also fashioned the "Hallelujah" bonnet for female soldiers.

It was a time of high infant mortality when Catherine had her family. In Britain, one child in three died at or soon after birth. Yet Catherine did not bury one of her eight children. She told them at a young age, "You are not in this world for yourself. You have been sent for others." Seven of her eight children became active in the Army.

Catherine was between meetings when she confessed she had a painful lump on her breast. The diagnosis was cancer. She preached her last sermon on June 21, 1888.

Catherine Booth triumphed over childhood illnesses, helped her husband establish the Salvation Army, bore eight children in eleven years, and faced the "female ministry" dispute of the day. She became a successful evangelist, paving the way for women in the Salvation Army to serve equally with men.

This Army "lassie" never received a rank in the organization. She was simply known as "Mother to an Army." The brass plaque on Catherine Booth's coffin rightfully described her: MORE THAN CONQUEROR.

What an example this heroine of the faith provides for us! As believers in Christ, we will also face persecutions, illnesses, and death. The Bible assures us, however, that like Catherine Booth, we will overcome. Surrounded by Jesus' love and with *His* courage, we are more than conquerors.

TERESA OF AVILA

Reformer, Mystic (1515–82)

*I want to know Christ and the power of his resurrection
and the fellowship of sharing his sufferings,
becoming like him in his death.*
PHILIPPIANS 3:10 NIV

As Teresa, a sixteenth-century Carmelite nun, sought God in prayer, she became more aware of errors in the church—and starting with her order, she sought to bring reform to the entire Christian world of that time.

Teresa was raised in a Christian home in Spain. Influenced by her father, who studied religious books, she became interested in spiritual matters. When her mother died, Teresa's father placed her in a convent. At age twenty, she took vows as a nun. A short time later, she became seriously ill. When restored to health, Teresa said her healing was miraculous.

Teresa lived an austere life, sleeping on straw, eating no meat, and wearing coarse garments. She held herself to a strict standard for Christian conduct and was known to punish herself for small infractions. This changed when she read Augustine's *Confessions,* and as he had heard God's voice, Teresa claimed the Lord also spoke to her.

While Teresa didn't seek ecstatic experiences as she sought God in prayer, she received visions and raptures, which she recorded in a journal. When she shared the mystical happenings with friends, they criticized and shunned her, claiming she was demon possessed.

Teresa wrote five books. In *Interior Castle*, she described the progress of a soul toward union with God. She said prayer is "a friendly conversation with One who loves us," and stated there are four stages of spiritual meditation. First, one must quiet the inner self. Second, a seeker becomes one with God by concentrating on His will. Third comes the repose or joy of the soul. Fourth, Teresa claimed the person experiences his soul's union with God, which she called a spiritual marriage. She wrote much on "mental prayer," which she described as taking time to frequently commune with God.

When Teresa was in her forties, she received a vision of the crucified Christ and became concerned for the spiritual state of the nuns in the Carmelite order, encouraging them to put God first and depend on Him for all their needs. She acknowledged abuses and coldness in the church, and she was a leader in the Counter Reformation. Church authorities, threatened by her ministry, strongly opposed Teresa and called her a restless gadabout. When the pope investigated Teresa's activities, he ruled in her favor.

Through prayer and study, Teresa enjoyed an intimate relationship with God—and He revealed His glory to her. We *can* know God and enjoy His presence. This deep friendship comes as we commune with Him day after day.

MARY SLESSOR

Missionary (1848–1915)

Pray about everything.
Tell God what you need, and thank him for all he has done.
If you do this, you will experience God's peace.
PHILIPPIANS 4:6–7 NLT

Most Europeans who stepped foot on Calabar's soil quickly died from disease or violence. Yet for thirty-eight years, missionary Mary Slessor shared the gospel with the people in this African country. She attributed her survival to prayer—prayer for strength to live with chronic malaria day after day while confronting the spiritual darkness in a land where the gospel had never before penetrated.

Mary was born in Scotland. As a child, she often cowered in fear when her father returned home in a drunken rage. Her mother, a Christian, worked in a textile mill. At age eleven, Mary began working part-time while attending school. Four years later, she worked ten hours a day at a loom.

Through the efforts of an elderly widow, Mary accepted Christ at a young age. Another bright spot in her life was her church, where she taught a Sunday school class, worked at a mission, and helped in street services where she was exposed to rough street gangs. Although Mary didn't know it, these experiences were preparing her for life in Calabar.

With the death of missionary David Livingstone, waves of missionary fervor swept across Great Britain—and in 1876, with no formal training, twenty-eight-year-old Mary sailed for Africa.

Calabar's swamps, infested with poisonous snakes and alligators, were the breeding ground for deadly fevers. The natives practiced human sacrifice. Twins were considered a curse and swiftly murdered or buried alive. Neighboring tribes often fought and made slaves of their captives or ate them. For centuries, white men had not traveled more than a few miles inland.

Mary was assigned to Duke Town, where she quickly learned the Efik language. She taught, preached, and nursed the sick. Yet she longed to push inland. The mission board, however, thought the move too dangerous for a single woman. Finally, in 1886, she established a mission in Old Town and "went native." She ate what the natives ate and lived in a mud hut infested with roaches, rats, and snakes.

Mary preached, established schools, and acted as a circuit preacher, traveling to remote villages to share the gospel. Rum was king in Old Town. It was used in trade and given to babies. Often Mary was the only sober person for miles around. When she heard of the birth of twins, she'd walk hours in torrential rains through dense jungles to find the abandoned babies. Soon several children lived under her roof.

In 1888, Mary again pushed inland. At Okoyong, the British government recognized her influence and appointed her vice counsel of the territory. In this capacity, "White Ma," as she was called, acted as a judge in the many disputes between tribes. It was a ludicrous sight: Mary, barefoot, wearing a loose dress, her short red hair flaming, calmly holding court to determine the fate of a native. When the decision was left up to Mary, the person survived. But before she came to this part of Africa, many innocent natives were buried alive or suffered death by flogging for minor crimes.

During one of Mary's furloughs to the coast, she met and fell in love with missionary Charles Morrison. She accepted his proposal of marriage on the condition that he would work with her in Okoyong. When his health failed, making it impossible for him to move inland, Mary broke their engagement. Her call to the work was her priority.

Mary saw little progress in establishing a church and viewed her efforts as preparation for future missionary work. In 1903, she conducted her first baptismal service when she baptized eleven people. Seven were her adopted children.

How did Mary survive the years in Calabar? She later testified that her life was "one daily, hourly record of answered prayer, for physical health, guidance, for errors, dangers, food, and total peace."

How do we survive the rigors of our godless society? *Prayer.* As prayer was the answer for Mary Slessor, so prayer will help us overcome physical weaknesses, temptations, fears, and evil, all the while keeping us in God's perfect peace.

THEODORA

Christian Empress (508–48)

By me kings reign and rulers make laws that are just;
by me princes govern, and all nobles who rule on earth.
PROVERBS 8:15–16 NIV

Theodora was born in Cyprus. Encouraged by her family, she became an actress, although it was considered an immoral occupation at that time. After she was mistreated and abandoned by the man she lived with, she converted to Christianity. In 525, she married Justinian I. Two years later, he became emperor of the Byzantine Empire.

Theodora successfully reigned with her husband for thirty-eight years. During this time the couple worked to restore Constantinople to its former glory. They rebuilt bridges and aqueducts and erected twenty-five churches. When a rebellion arose to overthrow the empire, Theodora persuaded her husband to defend the city rather than flee. Justinian, filled with new courage, soon crushed the enemy and restored order.

Concerned for women's causes, Theodora instituted the death penalty for rape. She forbade the killing of a wife who had committed adultery and passed laws to outlaw prostitution. With the closing of brothels, she founded a convent where the ex-prostitutes could live.

Because Theodora, a sixth-century empress, knew God, she made laws based on biblical truth. We are commanded to pray for our leaders so they, too, will make laws that uphold God's standard of righteousness and justice.

LOTTIE MOON

Missionary (1840–1912)

I plead with you to give your bodies to God.
Let them be a living and holy sacrifice. . . .
When you think of what he has done for you,
is this too much to ask?

ROMANS 12:1 NLT

As a young girl, Charlotte Digges Moon's interest in missions was stirred as her mother read missionary stories to her. Lottie attended a women's seminary and became one of the first Southern women to obtain a master's degree. When she heard a sermon on the text "Lift up your eyes, and look on the fields; for they are white already to harvest" (John 4:35 KJV), she determined to become a missionary.

In 1873, at age thirty-three, Lottie left plantation life in post–Civil War Virginia bound for China. She quickly learned the language and adopted Chinese dress. After accompanying fellow missionaries to outlying villages, she felt called as an evangelist. Instead, she was assigned to teach in a girls' school, which she considered "a folly and a waste."

Lottie was lonely in China. A Civil War chaplain had proposed marriage, but because he accepted the evolutionary theory of creation, she refused his offer.

A prolific letter writer, Lottie frequently wrote to American church women asking for help. When her pleas were not realized, Lottie purchased books and supplies with her own meager salary. Discouraged because of lack of funds and workers, on one occasion she wrote to the mission board, "I wonder how these things look in heaven. They certainly look very queer in China."

When she first began teaching Chinese women and children, they called her "The Old Devil Woman." As she nursed them through smallpox plagues and protected them in times of revolution, they changed her name to "The Heavenly Book Visitor."

In 1885, Lottie made a treacherous journey to an area where no woman missionary had ever been. Alone at Pingtu, she evangelized the area, and soon converts numbered in the hundreds. Four years later, she established a church.

Lottie wrote a letter in 1888 that changed the course of Southern Baptist missions: She asked the women of America to give a special Christmas offering to mission efforts. Thus began the now-famous Lottie Moon Christmas Offering.

Because of a revolution in 1912, the American council advised all missionaries to leave; yet Lottie stayed at her mission. As food became scarce, she gave all she had to Chinese believers. Weak, malnourished, and aided by a nurse, Lottie sailed for America. En route, she died in Japan.

Lottie once said, "I would that I had a thousand lives that I might give them to the women of China." As we ponder Christ's sacrifice on Calvary, total dedication to His cause is also the acceptable response for us to make.

NOTES

NOTES

NOTES

NOTES

NOTES

NOTES